# THE LIBRARY TREE

# THE
# LIBRARY TREE

How a Canadian woman brought the joy of reading
to a generation of African children

## DEBORAH COWLEY

GREAT PLAINS
PUBLICATIONS

Great Plains Publications gratefully acknowledges the financial support provided for its publishing program by the Government of Canada through the Canada Book Fund; the Canada Council for the Arts; the Province of Manitoba through the Book Publishing Tax Credit and the Book Publisher Marketing Assistance Program; and the Manitoba Arts Council.

Design & Typography by Relish Design Studio Inc.
Printed in Canada by Friesens

LIBRARY AND ARCHIVES CANADA CATALOGUING IN PUBLICATION

Cowley, Deborah, author
      The library tree : how a Canadian woman brought the joy
of reading to a generation of African children / Deborah Cowley.

ISBN 978-1-926531-83-0 (pbk.)

      1. Knowles, Kathy.  2. Children--Ghana--Library resources.
3. Children--Books and reading--Ghana.  4. Public libraries--Ghana.
5. Literacy programs--Ghana.  6. Ghana--Biography.  I. Title.

Z718.2.G48C69 2013      027.62'509667      C2013-904601-1

**ENVIRONMENTAL BENEFITS STATEMENT**

**Great Plains Publications** saved the following resources by printing the pages of this book on chlorine free paper made with 100% post-consumer waste.

| TREES | WATER | ENERGY | SOLID WASTE | GREENHOUSE GASES |
|---|---|---|---|---|
| 10 | 4,510 | 4 | 302 | 832 |
| FULLY GROWN | GALLONS | MILLION BTUs | POUNDS | POUNDS |

Environmental impact estimates were made using the Environmental Paper Network Paper Calculator 3.2. For more information visit www.papercalculator.org.

FSC
www.fsc.org
MIX
Paper from
responsible sources
FSC® C016245

*"It is my wish that the voice of the storyteller will never die in Africa, that all the children in the world may experience the wonder of books, and that they will never lose the capacity to enlarge their earthly dwelling place with the magic of stories."*

—NELSON MANDELA

*For Kathy, for inviting me to share this journey.*

# TABLE OF CONTENTS

## AUTHOR'S NOTE

I NEVER IMAGINED ON THAT DAY IN MARCH 2000 WHEN I LANDED AT Accra's Kotoka airport that my life would be changed forever.

I had come to Ghana to write an article for *Reader's Digest* about Kathy Knowles, a young Canadian woman who, I had heard, was something of a heroine to thousands of children in this West African country. I had travelled often to Africa as a freelance journalist but had never visited Ghana. Here was my chance.

I had first read about Kathy a few years earlier in a small column in the Toronto newspaper, *The Globe and Mail*. Back then, she had already raised enough money to build one very successful children's library in Ghana's capital, Accra, and had helped create more than 75 smaller ones around the country. I tried to find out more about her but with little success so I picked up the phone and arranged to meet her at Toronto airport just as she was leaving on one of her visits to Ghana. We spoke for barely an hour but I quickly sensed the charisma and compassion of this soft-spoken woman and I came away convinced that hers was a story worth telling. Happily, my editors agreed and soon after, I booked a flight to Ghana.

I had already read that Ghana was a former British colony and is sandwiched between the Ivory Coast and Togo in the bulge that is West Africa. It is about the size of Britain and, in 1957, was the first African country to gain its independence. The new nation's first president, Kwame Nkrumah, had promised hope and prosperity for the whole continent but the euphoria was short-lived. After a period of far-reaching successes, power went to his head and, in 1966, he was deposed in a coup and died in exile. There followed two decades of coups and counter-coups before the country began to enjoy relative stability. By the time I arrived in 2000, Ghana had embraced a working democracy.

It was already dusk when I stepped out of Accra's airport and faced complete pandemonium. The place shook with the sounds of pounding drums and rhythmic clapping. It turned out that one of my fellow passengers was a famous Ghanaian boxing champion returning home from a recent victory. I elbowed my way through the cheering mobs, searching for Kathy. Suddenly, I spotted her white face among the vast sea of black heads. She was waving frantically as she inched her way towards me.

I knew that Kathy, then just 45, had already done more in her short life than most people twice her age. What I did not know was how she managed to accomplish so much given the heat and humidity of this dusty African capital and all the uncertainties and challenges of daily life in this part of the world. I was soon to find out. In the days ahead, I was able to observe her skill in navigating the endlessly complex obstacles, her patience in the face of the most daunting bureaucracy, and a remarkable empathy with Africans. By the time I met her, she had already managed to transform the lives of thousands of Ghanaian children thanks largely to the libraries she had built in Accra and around the country.

At the airport, we climbed into a rickety, 14-year-old taxi for the ride into town. I looked around trying to make sense of this new city, now bathed in darkness, as Kathy outlined our plans for the next day. "I'll pick you up at 5 a.m. tomorrow morning. Is that okay?" she said, obviously expecting me to agree. She went on to explain that during my ten days in Ghana, we would visit many libraries and schools in Accra and would travel by car to see several others in different corners of the country.

She arrived at my small hotel the next morning promptly at 5 a.m. with the same taxi and Kofi, the driver. We gulped down a quick breakfast—a boiled egg and bread was all we could muster at that hour—and took off.

During the next week, we criss-crossed the country, sometimes on paved roads, more often on dusty, pot-holed ones that led to a remote library that Kathy had launched. We drove one ten hour stretch north to Tamale, then a sleepy town with more bicycles than cars, and wended our way across its surrounding plains to visit half a dozen village libraries. We followed the coastal road west, then pushed north into the mining region where more of Kathy's libraries had received her help. We travelled to the lush and scenic Volta Region on the eastern-most edge of Ghana, a sharp contrast to the noise and chaos of the capital.

Back in Accra, we stopped by several government schools which Kathy had already visited. And we spent time with hundreds of children who were enjoying the two libraries she had, by then, built in the city.

The reception was the same at every stop: a gaggle of excited youngsters would welcome us like royalty, greeting 'Madam Katty' with a song, a poem, a bouquet of wildflowers. Within minutes of our arrival, Kathy would perch herself on a stool, take out a book and read a story while the children sat on floor mats or at their desks, enthralled.

She would then ask them to name their favourite storybooks. Dozens of eager hands would shoot up as they shouted out their different titles. "That's *wonderful*," beamed Kathy. "A year ago, these children had never seen a storybook," she explained to me proudly. "In fact, many of them could barely read. Just look at them now!"

This was the pattern for my full ten-day stay. Up at 5 and home by 11. Lunching on roadside snacks of roasted plantains or deep fried yams and sharing in the delight of so many kids who, thanks to 'Madam Katty,' had come under the spell of books. By the end of my stay, it had become abundantly clear that Kathy, in her gentle and modest way, had touched the hearts of many.

I returned to Canada and wrote my story. It was published in 2001 and garnered an enthusiastic response. As the weeks passed, something about Kathy's story kept nagging me. I couldn't let it go. I could not get out of my head the image of all those children who became so excited by their discovery of books. Nor could I stop thinking about the remarkable Ghanaian people I had met—their kindness, their warmth, their generosity of spirit—often living against the most overwhelming odds.

I thought again about Kathy and her genuine passion for what she was doing. I thought about her dogged determination to bring about change and the wise and thoughtful way that she ran her tiny grassroots organization. It was one of the most effective and far-reaching aid projects I had seen and it was all done on a tiny budget and with the most minimum administration costs. I decided to offer to help in any way I could.

Two years later, Kathy asked me to travel with her back to Ghana to give her a hand with a new library project. I jumped at the chance. More library visits. More delighted children. More moving tributes to our 'Canadian angel.' Back in Canada, I had begun to help with fundraising, correspondence, grant proposals, anything Kathy threw my way. I continued to be involved on both continents until a surprise request came from Kathy in 2006. Would I like to spend three months in Ghana to oversee a project that she wanted to complete before the visit that fall of Canada's Governor General Michaëlle Jean? The timing would be good. Earlier that year, my husband had died after a lengthy illness so Kathy's offer would provide a welcome distraction and a modicum of healing. The decision was an easy one. It had become clear to me that, slowly, almost imperceptibly, Ghana was taking over my life. I accepted the challenge.

In November 2012, I made my fifteenth trip to Ghana. When friends back home ask me what I do when I am there, it is hard to convey the daily demands we face, the pace we keep, the problems we encounter and the people we meet. But I know that when I sink into bed each night, I consider myself fortunate to be part of this exciting project and to have found such a rewarding challenge to fill my retirement years.

I am now answering another challenge with this book: to record a story that began more than twenty years ago under a tree in a garden in Accra. By sharing Kathy's story, it is my hope that more and more people—especially those in Africa—will learn from her example and that their children and grandchildren will grow up knowing the joy of reading.

—DEBORAH COWLEY, OTTAWA, JUNE 2013

# INTRODUCTION

GHANA'S CAPITAL, ACCRA, IS A NOISY, CONGESTED CITY OF 2.5 MILLION. Hugging the equator, it is hot and humid most of the year with daytime temperatures that rarely drop below a stifling 32 degrees. While the pace of human life ebbs and flows, the speed and frenzy on the roads rarely lets up. Sirens scream throughout the day. Cars belch out black diesel fumes into the already-polluted air while eager teenagers thread their way through the stalled vehicles hawking everything from dish rags to dog leashes, balloons to binoculars. Snaking precariously around them, dilapidated taxis jostle with private cars for space on the crowded roads.

Life on the side of the road is no calmer. Swarms of schoolchildren sporting yellow and brown uniforms and carrying bulging school bags saunter home while women weave their way through the crowds, balancing everything on their heads from sewing machines or sacks of charcoal, stalks of sugar cane, even a kitchen sink. The humidity from the nearby sea hangs heavily in the air and the smell of spicy food cooked over an open fire permeates most corners.

There are a few pockets of tranquility in this frenetic city, away from the sounds of blaring horns and screeching brakes. One is North Ridge, a leafy corner of the capital bordering the better-known Osu area. The relatively quiet streets are lined with century-old Neem trees, their arched branches providing a shady canopy for pedestrians. Bougainvillea blossoms in splashes of pink, purple and orange tumble from high concrete walls.

It was here, in April 1990, that Canadian Kathy Knowles was living with her husband, John and their four small children—Kaitlan aged eight, Sophie aged five, Alastair aged three, and baby Akos, then six months old. They had arrived in Ghana eight months earlier where John had accepted a job as an accountant with a Canadian mining company. They had found a large colonial-style house in North Ridge with a two acre garden ablaze with flowering shrubs and trees.

Kathy had always enjoyed storybooks as a child and she had brought along some of her favourites to read to her children. Once they had settled into their new home, they had befriended some of the neighbourhood youngsters who would drop by their house after school. Kathy noticed that these children were fascinated by her books and she quickly learned that they were a complete novelty for them and something they didn't have in their own homes. As she watched them eagerly leaf through the pages, she had an idea: why not start a small library in her garden for these few children and offer them a chance to enjoy her storybooks?

First, she needed more books. She found a few in the local shops but she soon discovered that good quality storybooks suitable for African children were very scarce in Accra. She then learned from a Canadian friend that some donated books had arrived from Canada and were waiting for clearance at the port. These would provide a good starting-point for her venture while she waited for more to arrive from family and friends in Canada.

It was a hot and steamy afternoon when Kathy filled a basket with a few of her books and carried it down the steps into her garden. George, her cook's son, was the first to turn up. Becky and Philip, children of the tailor and his wife who lived next door, arrived next, followed by Grace and her twin brothers, Richard and Richmond, who also lived nearby.

As Kathy stepped into the garden, she looked more like a svelte teenager than a 34-year-old mother of four. Atop her slim figure was a mop of bushy, brown shoulder-length hair and she exuded an easygoing, laid-back disposition. She appeared to be oblivious to the oppressive heat as she placed her basket on the ground, pulled up a stool and sat under the spreading branches of a scarlet Flamboyant tree. The six children sat in front of her and listened, wide-eyed, as she opened the first book and began to read. *"Once upon a time, there lived an unhappy young girl called Cinderella..."*

She finished the book, then read another and another holding each one up to show the children the pictures. They sat silently, eyes fixed firmly on the pages as she led them through the tales of the Gingerbread Man and Pooh Bear. They snickered at the escapades of Curious George and cheered when Cinderella met her handsome prince.

The garden story time lasted less than an hour. By the time Kathy turned the last page of the last book, the children were so keen that she let each one borrow two books which they could take home. Since most of them had never had a storybook in their house, she felt that this would give them a sense of ownership, if only for a while. She kept a record of the borrowed books and made sure the children knew they should return them the next week and in good condition.

The six children came to the garden every Thursday afternoon. More books soon arrived and, as Kathy's supply grew larger and her basket heavier, she found a carpenter to make a cabinet with wheels so she could fill it with books and roll it outside.

"That was it," she said. "Just six kids under a tree. It was all so simple." Kathy had no way of knowing that this small initiative was about to transform her life.

NEWS OF KATHY'S STORYTELLING CIRCLE SPREAD RAPIDLY AROUND the neighbourhood. Each library afternoon, more children spotted the reading circle from the road and would walk into the garden and ask if they could join. They then brought their friends, who brought their friends.

As the group expanded, Kathy thought she would branch out. She began by teaching the children a few simple songs. One of the most popular was "The wheels on the bus go round and round..." The youngsters caught on quickly and sang along, clapping out the rhythm of each verse. The pace quickened and they all collapsed into giggles.

Kathy thrived on the excitement of her garden library. "Apart from the fun I had with all those kids," she says, "this gave me such a wonderful link with Ghanaians. Many expatriates live for months before they meet members of the local community. But here I was, plugged right in. It was really neat."

It wasn't long before many people in the community—and far beyond—knew what was happening in this Canadian woman's garden. The number of children continued to grow until one day, Kathy counted 70 in the garden! They sat wherever they could find a spot. Some squatted on the steps of the veranda while others found a patch on the lawn as they listened to the stories. "It was obvious that this was something these children missed in their lives and which they adored," Kathy said. "But 70 children?" She shook her head in amazement.

It was not surprising that storybooks were so foreign to these children. Back then, books were prohibitively expensive so the majority of Ghanaians could never afford them. Also, the government school system was not conducive to reading. Children whose parents could afford school fees had to share the few available textbooks with their classmates. Storybooks were considered a luxury and were rarely relevant to the curriculum while teachers taught largely by rote with the children repeating every word like robots. Furthermore there were no creative activities of any sort—no storybooks, no art materials, nothing in the classroom to stimulate children's curiosity or to enable their imaginations to stir.

Then there were the legions of children who were unable to attend school at all. School fees were then obligatory and beyond the reach of many parents as were the smaller sums for uniforms, shoes and schoolbags. These youngsters simply stayed at home, turned to begging or roamed the streets where they were easily lured into petty crime.

As more and more children turned up in Kathy's garden, she began to realize that the whole thing was becoming unmanageable. How could she meet the needs of the increasing number of children who wanted to join her circle and still keep some order? She had seen for herself how important books had become to those already turning up but what about all the others? She thought long and hard. "I must find a way to give more children the chance to discover the excitement of books."

# CHAPTER 1

## New Beginnings

IT WAS LESS THAN A YEAR EARLIER, IN JANUARY 1989, THAT KATHY AND her husband John were recuperating from the Christmas celebrations in their rural Ontario home, west of Toronto. They had lived there for the past three years and enjoyed the freedom and challenges of country life.

One winter's morning that January, the two were eating breakfast when John happened to spot an ad in *The Globe and Mail*. It listed a job for an accountant with Sikaman, a Canadian-owned gold mining company. The position would initially be for two years and would be located in Ghana, a country in West Africa. John was then working in a nine-to-five job with an accounting firm in nearby Toronto but somewhere in the back of his mind there was clearly a hint of restlessness creeping in. "I don't know what prompted me to apply for that job," he said. "I suppose I was just curious. But I was also woefully ignorant about Africa and I knew precious little about Ghana. Ghana, Guinea, Guinea-Bissau. They all sounded the same to a Canadian from Toronto."

Neither he nor Kathy had actually spoken about moving abroad, let alone to Africa, but John was intrigued by the idea so he mailed off an application. Within weeks, he was amazed to receive an offer. "I hesitated for days to tell Kathy about the job," he admitted. "I was sure she would say 'no'."

When he finally told Kathy, he was surprised that at first she greeted the idea with enthusiasm. She too admitted knowing little about Africa and would have been hard-pressed to find Ghana on a map. However, as the idea began to sink in, different concerns sprung to mind. How would her children react to the idea? How would they adjust to such a different environment? Would there be suitable schools for them? What about the health issues the family would face, especially with such young children?

She also wasn't sure what she would do with her time. She saw motherhood as a full-time vocation for the early years but what would she do when the children were older? She had trained and worked as a paediatric nurse and had volunteered with various helping agencies but she had no idea what sort of opportunities would be available for her in Ghana.

However, the more she thought and read about Ghana, the more she became excited about the idea of a new adventure. She had assumed that Ghana was much like other African nations that were enmeshed in civil war, run by power-hungry despots or prone to massive corruption. But she quickly learned that, though the country had come through some difficult times, it was now relatively stable. She was also relieved to learn that since Ghana had once been a British colony, English was widely spoken.

John too did some fast reading before accepting the offer. He scanned a map of West Africa, the large hump on the top left corner of the continent, and found Ghana, a long thin country roughly the shape of a shoe-box that sits squarely on the Atlantic Ocean. It is wedged between the small sliver of Togo to the east and the much larger Ivory Coast to the west, both French-speaking countries. Accra, the capital, faces the ocean and lies close to the equator so it enjoys a constant and hot climate, hovering around 32 degrees most of the year.

John also learned that the country had been known as the Gold Coast when it was a British colony but at independence in 1957 it had taken the name "Ghana"—meaning "warrior king" from the days of the ancient Ghanaian empire that existed in the 8th to 11th centuries. It seemed that the country was rich in natural resources—cocoa, timber, palm oil and the all-important gold were in abundance. He also learned that of a population then of 15 million, half of the people were under the age of 16. Though the official language was English, there were more than 75 different languages and dialects spoken around the country.

Ghana's post-independence history had been a turbulent one, but by the time John Knowles had given up his accounting job in Toronto that May, things were relatively calm. So the decision was made. They were off to Ghana.

John left first to find accommodation for the family while Kathy stayed behind to rent the house and pack up the children. They were all too young to understand this big change in their lives but their parents had read them stories about Africa and treated the whole thing as an exciting new adventure.

Finally, the big day arrived and, on August 8, 1989, Kathy and the children set out on their journey. There were many tears as they said goodbye to family members at the airport, but they were already starting to look forward to the new chapter in their lives. As they boarded the plane for Ghana, Kathy not only had the three excited children clamouring for her attention during the long journey: she was also seven and a half months pregnant.

THE SEVEN HOUR FLIGHT CARRIED THE FAMILY ACROSS THE ATLANTIC to Amsterdam where they boarded another plane and flew a further six hours straight south. Looking out the window, Kathy could spot the green fields of France, then the choppy waters of the Mediterranean and finally, the northern coast of Africa. From then on, it was all sand as they flew over the vast expanse of the Sahara desert with its rippled dunes gleaming in the sun. Finally, the plane landed in Accra's Kotoka International Airport. The terminal was then housed in a small and simple building, vastly different from the present ultra-modern facility.

The minute Kathy stepped off the plane into the noisy, crowded terminal, she felt completely overwhelmed. The frenzy, the smells of the tropics, and the high humidity were almost suffocating. Added to all this was the scorching heat.

She flinched as the noise and chaos swirled around her. The children were hot and tired and frightened by the crowds. She was tired too, but needed to keep her composure so she could hold onto the children, navigate the lengthy immigration procedure, locate her bags, fend off the persistent offers of help and hopefully, find John. As she wheeled her top-heavy trolley out into the melee, she suddenly saw him elbowing his way through the crowd towards her. After an emotional reunion, he packed the family into the company car and drove into town.

By then it was dark, so Kathy could see little more than an eerie outline of the buildings they passed. When they drove along the Nima highway, the only lights were the flickering lanterns from the roadside kiosks. The sounds, the smells, the heat—it was all so different from her home in Canada half a world away.

The house John had found to rent was not yet ready for them so the family spent their first two weeks squeezed into a single room above John's office. Finally, they were able to move into their own home at 15 Osu Avenue in North Ridge. It was a handsome colonial-style building surrounded by a beautiful garden. Its centrepiece was a large Flamboyant tree, its arched branches laden with brilliant red flowers.

Kathy faced many challenges as she tried to come to grips with her new surroundings. But helping the children adjust to their strange new life was the first priority. She and John decided on an American international school for Kaitlan and Sophie, but the girls were both apprehensive about starting a new school. Alastair settled in happily at the Little Flower Montessori School, a pre-school program attended largely by Ghanaian children.

Next, they had to furnish their large house. They used an office car to comb the city to search for appliances and second-hand furniture from families leaving Ghana or to have cane furniture made for the house, the cheapest alternative to buying ready-made items. Kathy also visited the bustling market to buy material to make curtains and to stock up on local foods. She found that the banks and government offices were mostly located in the downtown area while the edges of Accra were a maze of low-slung houses. Beyond that, the city appeared to stretch forever, its fringes blending into wall-to-wall villages with roadside stalls selling everything from food to cell phones, toothpaste to pirated cassette tapes. Sandwiched between the stalls, small shops advertised their wares with signboards that announced 'Ever Merciful Photos,' 'Keep Smiling Dental Clinic,' 'Heaven Knows Beauty Care' and 'Almighty Plumbing Works.'

It was several weeks before they finally managed to buy a car and even later, hired Frank Mensah to be their driver. It was he who drove the children to school each morning, a journey through heavy traffic and construction that took an hour each way. To reach the school, they passed through Nima, one of the largest slums in Accra. Kathy remembers feeling pangs of guilt to see so much poverty, especially when she and her family were living in relative luxury. However, Kathy did have to learn how manage the time-consuming shopping and cooking for the family—a task that was becoming more difficult since she was expecting her fourth child in less than a month.

Her first big test came early. Barely two weeks after the family's arrival, five-year-old Sophie came down with a chest infection and an alarmingly high fever. She stopped eating and became so weak her parents had to carry her everywhere.

Kathy contacted a local paediatrician who treated Sophie for pneumonia but she didn't respond to the medication. They returned for more tests and the child turned out to have a serious case of malaria, the major cause of death in Africa. The family was completely numbed by the experience—and was relieved when Sophie recovered after nine harrowing days.

Foreigners in Ghana typically have household help and the company provided funds for some of that support but it was Kathy and John's job to find it. This was a foreign concept for them since help in Canada was neither affordable nor necessary. But with a new baby on the horizon, a large house to run and the daily challenges of food shopping and meal preparation, they decided that extra help would be welcome. After a long search, they managed to hire a cook, John Otumfo. He was a good cook and loved the children but it soon became clear that he was also an alcoholic. Kathy discovered this one evening when they had invited friends to dinner and the man the family called 'John Cook' turned up completely drunk. Kathy gave him an ultimatum: if he didn't stop drinking, he would have to leave. Not surprisingly, it happened again. Kathy remembers, "I said 'That's it.' John Cook cried and I cried, and off he went."

John Cook returned later, looking sheepish, and told Kathy that he wanted to come back so she gave him another chance. "He never gave up drinking, but the children adored him and he had become such part of our family that we just couldn't let him go."

Then there was Kabore, the night watchman from Burkina Faso who sat on the veranda with a bow and arrow by his side and paper in hand trying to choose the winning lotto numbers. To manage the large garden that included both flowers and vegetables, Kathy first hired Steven, then Joseph, a second gardener. They rounded out the household with the purchase of a golden lab puppy which John named Wellington, after the British general.

THROUGH ALL THE FLURRY OF SETTLING INTO HER NEW LIFE, KATHY was growing increasingly aware that her due date was fast approaching. She had already made inquiries about the state of Ghanaian hospitals and found them seriously understaffed, dirty and badly equipped. She tried other private facilities but learned that an anaesthetist was not always available which she felt was important in case she required a caesarean section. Friends urged her to return home or fly to Europe to have her baby but she was reluctant to leave Ghana and her family so soon after they had arrived.

Through a chance encounter with a new friend, Sylvia Traboulsi, she learned about a hospital with a good reputation in a small village called Battor, an hour-and-a-half drive east of Accra. The Battor Catholic Hospital was a mission hospital run by a religious order of German nuns. It came highly recommended—except for the fact that they only had generator-powered electricity twice a day. Kathy visited the hospital and met Sister Edgitha Gorges, the nun in charge. It turned out that she was a fully-trained gynaecologist and could do a caesarean section with a local anaesthetic if necessary. This was good news. Another staff member, Sister Margit Ohmacht, turned out to be Kathy's blood type—Rh negative—which was also reassuring. If by any chance she started haemorrhaging and needed blood, Sister Margit would be there as a blood donor.

IT WAS A SUNDAY AFTERNOON IN LATE SEPTEMBER, A SCANT SIX WEEKS after arriving in Ghana, that Kathy was sewing curtains for the dining room when she felt her first contractions. She phoned John, rang the caregiver who she had arranged to stay with the children, packed up her overnight bag and prepared to leave for the hospital. While she waited for John, she put the finishing touches on the curtains.

Since they were heading into the countryside and they still did not have their car, John's boss lent him his Nissan Patrol 4-wheel drive for the 70 kilometre journey. They left the house at 4 p.m. At first, it seemed like an easy drive with little traffic. However, it was the height of the rainy season so the roads were wet and muddy.

They were about ten kilometres from the hospital and it was already getting dark when they turned off the main highway onto a smaller dirt road. The rains had turned it into a sea of potholes filled with water. John zigzagged his way around the potholes, then swerved to avoid a big puddle in the middle of the road when suddenly, the car skidded off the shoulder, sank deep down into a rice paddy and the wheels got firmly and solidly stuck.

Kathy's contractions were still fairly mild so she remained in the car while John jumped out and pushed. The car wouldn't budge. About 20 passers-by stopped to help. They tried pushing as well, all knee deep in mud. Still no luck. Kathy and John thought carefully about their next move. Kathy's contractions were starting to get stronger and more regular so she knew she must get to the hospital quickly. There were no other cars on the road so when a large tro-tro (a van that serves as a bus) came along full of passengers, John flagged it down. The driver got out and he too tried to move the car without success. Kathy was becoming more and more worried so asked him if he would drive her to the hospital. The man paused, looking apprehensive. They negotiated a price, he finally agreed and offered her the front seat. She suggested that John stay with the car. She was sure that help would arrive soon since he had already requested that a tipper truck (a dump truck) come to the rescue. As Kathy climbed out of the car, she almost tripped over a large frog hopping around the floor of the front seat.

By the time she got into the tro-tro, Kathy was in so much pain, she could hardly breathe. It was pitch dark and she was sitting in a van filled with people she had never seen before.

They finally reached the hospital and Kathy climbed out while the driver hovered by nervously. They tried the gate, but it was locked. Finally, after what felt like ages, one of the nuns arrived and opened the gate. She took one look at Kathy, helped her into a wheelchair and rushed her straight into the delivery room where she met Sister Edgitha. "I remember taking off my sandals which were thick with mud and Sister Edgitha bent over and gently washed my feet. It reminded me of the biblical story of Christ washing the feet of his disciples. I found that so symbolic."

Less than 15 minutes later, Kathy gave birth to a healthy baby girl. They named her Madeleine Elizabeth and the nuns added the name 'Akosua' to the birth document which, in Ghana, means 'a Sunday-born girl.' She is still called Akosua, or Akos for short.

Meanwhile, John had finally been able to get help from the tipper truck which hauled his car out of the mud. He sped to the hospital and arrived about 9 p.m. covered in mud. He donned a hospital gown and arrived in the birthing room—a scant three minutes late. He walked in and found the nurse holding the new baby by her feet. It was the only birth he had missed.

Kathy described the day in a letter to her family. "The whole birth experience was really a memorable event. I can still see John and about ten others knee-deep in mud under a star-lit sky trying to push the vehicle out of the mud. The next day when we left the clinic, John waved to the many local people who had helped us out.

"And what was really neat was that the nuns presented me with this beautiful cactus flower. It was called 'Queen of the Night' and it only blooms for a few hours one night a year. The flower is about four inches in diameter and contains 50 off-white petals. Would you believe that the plant began to flower the very night that Akosua was born? I felt that the flower not only symbolized the miracle of birth but it was a perfect omen.

"It was exciting to be in the hospital through the night. I could hear so many sounds of tropical birds and at about 5 a.m., the nuns began singing hymns in the nearby Catholic Church. Then when I got up the next day, my friend Sylvia arrived with a bottle of champagne to celebrate the big event."

The next morning, John drove home to pick up the other children and bring them to the hospital to meet their new baby sister. He also seized the chance to send a message to the family in Canada and place a birth notice in *The Globe and Mail*. "John, Kathy, Kaitlan, Sophie, Alastair warmly welcome Akosua Madeline Elizabeth, born Sept. 24, 1989, 7 pounds 4 oz. Thanks to many who tried to pull our truck from the mud, the tro-tro driver who drove Kathy to the hospital, the tipper truck driver who did pull the car out and the nuns of the Battor Catholic Hospital, Ghana, West Africa for their wonderful treatment."

That afternoon, Kathy wrapped her new daughter in a light blanket, said goodbye to the hospital staff and travelled back home.

## CHAPTER 2

# *Her First Big Challenge*

LIFE WAS GOOD FOR THE KNOWLES FAMILY AND THEY SOON CAME TO love their adopted country. They found Ghanaians warm and friendly and always hospitable. "Even those who have very little are more than willing to share," said Kathy.

Once Kathy had settled the children into their new schools, she began to meet many friends, mostly those with small babies. Her parents visited that first year and her mother Beth ('Ginny' to the children) noticed at once that her daughter had already become a part of the local community. The children too settled easily into their new surroundings. During Beth's visit, Alastair returned from school one afternoon and proudly showed her a photograph of his class in which his was the only white face. Holding it up for his grandmother to see, he asked her, in all seriousness, "Ginny, can you find me?"

With the household under control and the ever-vigilant and caring 'John Cook' keeping a close eye on the new baby, Kathy decided to put her nursing training to use and accepted a part-time job as a nurse at the Canadian High Commission. Two mornings a week, she helped give vaccinations to the Canadian staff, dealt with any small medical concerns of the local Ghanaian employees and made referrals to recommended doctors. She enjoyed moving back into the nursing world and the friends she made through the job.

By this time, she had come to know her own household staff better and decided to use a portion of the earnings from her job to offer them some type of education. 'John Cook' opted for piano lessons but soon found he didn't have enough time to practise. Frank, the driver, attended Saturday morning classes to learn how to repair cooling systems. Stephen, the gardener, enrolled in English courses and Joseph, the second gardener, learned tailoring. They all took these lessons very seriously and Kathy enjoyed following their progress.

KATHY WAS NOW BUSIER THAN EVER, BALANCING HER NEW JOB AND caring for her children, especially the new baby. However, she was determined to keep up her Thursday afternoon reading circles in the garden. The children kept clamouring for these story time sessions so she couldn't let them down. To help ease the load, she decided to hire a housekeeper to assist with the housework. Fortune smiled the day that Joanna Felih (Fee-lay), a shy young woman of 23, turned up for an interview. She had come from a small village in the Volta Region on the eastern-most edge of Ghana. When her father died, she had to drop out of school and look for work to help support her family. She travelled to Accra and learned from her sister that Kathy was looking for household help. Kathy liked her on their first meeting and agreed to hire her on a part-time basis.

Joanna started at once. At first, she worked just two hours a day helping with the cleaning. Then Kathy increased it to three hours a day and after a few weeks, Joanna was working full-time. "From the very beginning, I felt so much a part of that family," she recalls. "I remember sitting with Kathy doing some mending and, even though this was very different from where I had come from, Kathy made me feel so comfortable and completely at home."

Kathy's reading circles had begun to grow and Joanna watched in amazement as Kathy took one book after another from her basket and read to the children. Storybooks were completely new to Joanna and she was surprised to see this white woman doing so much to help the Ghanaian children. She watched the children every Thursday afternoon sitting in the garden listening to stories and singing songs and saw how much they loved it. Occasionally, Kathy would ask Joanna to tell the children some of her own African stories. "Storytelling was a strong tradition where I came from, so I really enjoyed doing that," said Joanna.

Every week, more and more children streamed through the gate to enjoy the stories. Alison Hazledine, a New Zealander living in Ghana at the time, was one of many moms who brought their children to the garden. "My son, Tim, just adored those story sessions, as did all the other children," she recalls. "The popularity of Kathy's storytelling circles was quite astonishing. It was very quickly apparent that most of the neighbourhood children valued this event more than anything else in their life. In fact, every time we visited, the reading circle grew larger and larger."

Kathy didn't want to turn any children away but her garden library was clearly becoming unmanageable. Now that she had Joanna's help, she began thinking seriously of some way to accommodate more children.

She talked it over with John and they came up with an idea: they had a spare guest room on the ground floor of their house, a room they had already converted from a garage. Why not clear it out and turn it into a tiny library? It was not large—barely bigger than the size of a large car—but they decided to give it a try.

She and John removed all the bedroom furniture and painted the walls. Kathy found a carpenter to make a few small shelves and bought two brightly-coloured child-size tables and eight small chairs. Then she covered the bare walls with posters to add colour and wall-hangings of blue and white locally woven *kente* cloth to help absorb the sound.

All she needed now were more books. She wrote to her family and friends in Canada asking them to look for new and gently-used children's books and begged anyone visiting Ghana to tuck them into their suitcases. Her former church, Knox Presbyterian in Acton, Ontario, was the first to send money to cover some of the expenses and she used the salary from her nursing job to meet the rest. On all the family's trips back to Canada on her husband's semi-annual leave, she stuffed books into every corner of each child's suitcase.

It was Frank, the driver, who came up with a name for the new re-fitted garage/guest room. He suggested "Osu Library" after the name of their street. Joanna was already familiar with many of the children so Kathy asked her if she would like to take charge of the fledgling operation. Joanna was stunned. She hadn't even completed high school and admitted she knew nothing about running a library. "In fact," she said, "until I met Kathy, I didn't even know what a library was. But I was willing to try." Kathy had a uniform made for her—purple cotton with a white lace collar—and together, they put the final touches to the room. She arranged the books neatly on the shelves and the new pocket-sized library was ready for business.

THE TINY OSU LIBRARY OPENED ON MONDAY AND THURSDAY AFTERnoons from 3:30 pm to 5 p.m. On library days, Joanna sat under a mango tree near the library entrance and welcomed the children. She assigned each one a number and jotted down their name in a notebook. Within three months, 150 children had registered—almost all of them Ghanaian. Many of them lived in the neighbourhood but others crossed the city to attend. Some, from better-off families, arrived by car but most of them walked, some for miles, to share in the excitement. In fact, so many children wanted to take part that Kathy and Joanna decided to ask them to come on a designated day, half on Monday and the rest on Thursday.

Kathy enjoyed those early days as much as the children. She loved helping them to read or to write stories and shared in their delight of discovery. "From where I sat, I could see all the children lining up outside in front of Joanna's desk, eight or nine deep, waiting to come in. It was so heart warming."

Kathy then hired Noble, a young Ghanaian man, to teach the library members African drumming and dancing. "We loved the African dancing," recalls Becky, one of those first Ghanaian children. "It was so much fun watching Kathy's children learning to dance with us."

Kathy rounded out the team by employing Harry Lartey, a student from the University of Ghana, to read stories to the children. He was a handsome young Ghanaian with a big smile, was good with the children and a gifted storyteller. Best of all, he always turned up on time!

These regular story times were to become an important component in all Kathy's libraries. Very few children in Ghana had the chance to listen to stories. There was once a time in most villages when grandmothers sat around a fire in the evening telling stories to the children.

But those fireside storytelling days were disappearing with electrification in many villages and with families moving to urban centres. Kathy considers her story times to be a very special gift she can offer the children and she too seizes any chance she can to sit down and read to a child.

As she leafs through an album of photos from those early days, Kathy beams at the memories. "I just loved being in that little library and watching how the children responded to the stories and how they were drawn into the larger world of books. They just adored them, and their appetite for reading and writing was insatiable."

THE NEW LIBRARY WAS A REVELATION TO EVERYONE IN THE NEIGHBOUR-hood. Given that in 1990, the minimum monthly wage in Ghana was the equivalent of $18 US, many parents could not afford the required fees to send their children to school. The lucky ones who could attend school were not much better off: they rarely saw a book other than the dog-eared texts they had to share with their classmates. The few existing libraries, remnants from the colonial past, were dark and dreary facilities with shelves of tired and often unsuitable books.

Most of the young patrons of the Osu Library could understand English which is widely spoken in the former British colony. But the idea of a storybook was beyond what many could even imagine, so they had no idea how to handle them. Kathy and Joanna set strict guidelines from the start. They placed two basins of water, soap and a towel outside the room so that each child could wash and dry his hands before entering. Ghana is a humid and dusty country and this was one way of helping prolong the life of the books.

There were more rules to follow. Members had to remove their shoes before entering the library in order to keep the floors clean for story time. Joanna taught them how to turn the pages carefully from the top right-hand corner and not to damage the books. Before the library was up and running, Kathy and an aunt who was visiting from Canada sewed colourful cloth bags with hand-stencilled animal motifs and allowed the children to borrow one book to carry home in the bag. If they returned the book on time and in good condition, they could choose two more.

After ten 'returns' with a perfect record, they could borrow a 'red dot' book, one of the newest or most popular ones.

Each time a book was returned, Joanna checked every page and noted its condition under the child's name: clean, soiled, or spoiled. She asked minor offenders to write a short essay on How to Respect a Book. More serious offenders paid a small fine. "Above everything else," Kathy points out, "we wanted to teach the children to value the books."

THE MONTHS FLEW BY AND THE LIBRARY CONTINUED TO THRIVE WITH more children turning up every week. Kathy loved to watch the transformation in so many of the children and she was very relieved when John's company invited him to stay on for another two years. Joanna was quickly picking up many skills from Kathy: she learned how to handle large numbers of children, how to maintain discipline and how to organize the all-important story readings. "We had such a wonderful time," she recalled. "I was so happy working in that little library."

But what now? Kathy had introduced all these youngsters to reading but it was becoming impossible to keep up with the need in such cramped quarters. Every month brought more and more children and there was already a waiting list from many others who wished to join. She was always mindful of the fact that this was only a temporary arrangement since she had built the library into the family's rented accommodation.

Once again, she talked it over with John. They were both aware that John's contract would be ending in less than two years and they would need to leave their house which was home to the library when they returned to Canada. But what to do? Kathy hated to disappoint the children who had come to enjoy the place. As she watched them lining up at the gate each library afternoon, she realized that so many of them had come to love their library visits. She had seen how their reading had improved. She had heard parents report that their children's school grades had shot up, and best of all, she had seen, every single day, how much fun they had there. Night after night, she lay tossing in bed trying to figure out what to do next. "I knew I had to do something to keep the library going," she said. "I just wasn't sure what."

# CHAPTER 3

## *A Shipping Container Transformed*

KATHY SPENT MANY LONG HOURS TRYING TO THINK OF WAYS TO continue her library. She started by contacting everyone she knew who might have ideas about how to proceed but no one came up with an answer. She then decided to take matters into her own hands. She started by looking for a place to rent and day after day, she walked up and down the neighbouring streets hunting for somewhere that would be suitable for a small library. She approached the Ghana Commission on Children to see if she could rent space in their building. "Not possible," she was told. They didn't have room for a library. Two other buildings looked promising but one owner suddenly boosted the rent and the family who owned the other decided they needed the space. Again and again, she received the same negative reply.

She then decided it might be easier to look for a vacant piece of land and work from there. Another long search turned up nothing. "I never imagined it would be so difficult," she recalled. "The whole exercise required so much patience and persistence—what the Ghanaians call 'Go and Come'—and I didn't have much of that."

But despite her modesty, she did have patience and persistence . . . and plenty of it. Eventually the 'P and P,' as she called it, paid off. One day, completely by chance, she happened to meet a Ghanaian friend, Gloria Danquah, who worked as a paediatrician at the Police Hospital. Kathy shared her frustration with Gloria who said she would make inquiries at the police department to see if Kathy could put up a temporary structure on a piece of their land a few streets from their house in North Ridge. Kathy held her breath.

It was several days before she heard that the authorities agreed to allow her to place a temporary structure on a small parcel of dusty land tucked in behind the government State House. Better still, there would be no cost. Kathy assured them she would erect a building they would be proud of and she would plant bougainvillea shrubs around the premises. Gloria's only request was that she also plant some around the whole compound. "Of course," Kathy assured her.

Kathy was already familiar enough with Ghanaian bureaucracy to know that this was just the first step. She still needed to secure the necessary written permission to erect even a 'temporary' structure on the land. The question of land in Ghana is a complicated one. Any building project requires a convoluted set of permissions and Kathy knew it was important to get all the details of the agreement written down on paper.

She began by writing a letter to the appropriate authorities. There was no reply. She wrote again, and again. Still no answer. Undaunted, she pressed on. From one day to the next, she sat outside different government offices in the hopes of intercepting an official who could provide the required document. By early evening, she would return home empty-handed. She never knew whether it was the inefficiency of a highly bureaucratic system, or a lack of trust in this 'obruni', the Ghanaian term for whites. It could have been that they were expecting a bribe but she wasn't willing to give one. Whatever the case, she was getting nowhere. But Kathy was not one to give up easily. "Stubborn is the word, I guess," she said of herself. So she kept hammering away.

Finally, ages later, a man from the police department who lived behind the property, stepped in, listened to her case, made a few enquiries and managed to secure the elusive document. Kathy heaved a sigh of relief. It had taken two long months to obtain that vital piece of paper. At last, she was ready to move.

The agreement made it clear that the structure was considered 'temporary' so she needed something that could be moved if necessary. She thought the best answer would be to buy a used shipping container, the 40 feet long and eight feet wide boxes used to transport cargo. It would be relatively cheap and easy to move to the new site. She didn't think it would be a hard thing to find but she faced another road block. She made many inquiries and would get 'yes', then 'no,' then 'maybe.' Finally, after searching for weeks, she managed to locate a rusty container from a shipping company. It cost $1200 US.

Now that she had found the container, she needed to raise the money to buy it. She got on the phone and began canvassing local businesses in Ghana. She called everyone she could think of in Ghana and in Canada but quickly discovered that raising money was tougher than she had thought. Everyone wanted a guarantee that the library would be a success before handing over a donation and that wasn't possible. Slowly, very slowly, the money trickled in. Friends and family members in Canada helped. A few local businesses chipped in. To reach her target, she dipped into her own "personal fund"—savings from her job at the Canadian High Commission. Eventually, she had raised enough money to buy the container.

THE COMPANY DELIVERED THE CONTAINER TO THE PROPERTY AND Kathy, though completely inexperienced, jumped into the role of project manager. She hired a small contracting company to lay a cement foundation and the movers placed the container on the concrete platform. She then found a local welder (by the name of 'Dr. Iron') to raise the roof and cut out windows and a door, while an electrician installed ceiling fans and hooked up the electricity. A friend helped Kathy and Joanna lay down blue linoleum floor tiles and a carpenter installed louvered windows to let in light and air, built wooden shelves for the books and puzzles, racks for shoes and pegs for school bags.

Kathy then recruited students from the nearby School of Journalism and volunteers from Rotaract (the youth of Rotary) to paint the inside white and the outside a bright metallic blue—Kathy's favourite colour. When she tallied up all the costs of transforming the container, it worked out to be around $5000 US, more than she had budgeted for so once again, she used her own savings to finish the job. Finally, a friend with the Dutch Embassy made a donation to cover book purchases

The minute the paint was dry, Kathy and John moved all the tables and stools, the books and toys from their converted garage into the new library. With the help of the students, they then planted a small garden outside. They framed the door with two vibrant pink bougainvillea bushes—a flower that would become a signature of all Kathy's libraries. As promised, they dug in bougainvillea shrubs around the whole compound. They later installed 25 painted tree stumps in a shady part of the garden to provide outdoor sitting space for story time.

The new library was a scant eight feet wide and 40 feet long but it looked warm and welcoming. It had taken only a few weeks to transform the rusty container and the barren land around it into an attractive space and before long, there were colourful flowers blooming outside the building and dozens of excited children inside.

In those early days, even before the new library was up and running, it became clear that Kathy needed to raise more funds to move forward. Her mother, Beth Lennard, a businesswoman who runs the family's commercial real estate firm in Calgary, saw that it was time to register the project in Canada. In 1991, she arranged for the library effort to become an official charity with the name, Osu Children's Library Fund (OCLF), which allowed donors to receive tax receipts. "I knew that Kathy was spending a lot of her own money on this project and I also felt certain that this was just the beginning of her work," said Beth. "So I thought it was time to take this step to enable her to move ahead."

Two years later, in 1993, Kathy created a Ghanaian partner— the Osu Library Fund (OLF)—and recruited Florence Adjepong, a British educated Jamaican married to a Ghanaian, and Ghanaian Emma Amoo-Gottfried, who had attended school in Britain, to serve as the board of directors. Both these women were mothers of children who had been among the first library members in Kathy's garden on Osu Avenue. They were both hard-working and dedicated educators who would soon establish and head up two of the best private schools in Ghana for students from kindergarten to high school. In spite of their heavy workloads, they continued to provide a supportive presence for Kathy and Joanna over the years.

JOANNA HAD ALREADY PROVEN TO BE AN EXCELLENT LIBRARIAN SO Kathy had no hesitation in asking her to take charge of the new facility. "I could not think of anyone else in the world I would want to run my first real library," she said. "It was Joanna's passion for what she does that allowed us to move forward so quickly."

Kathy then submitted a request for a member of Ghana's National Service personnel to help Joanna. These are Ghanaian university graduates who are obliged to volunteer for one year after graduation, a type of 'pay back' for their relatively low university fees. Who should turn up but a somewhat bewildered young man named Michael Moffat who stepped through the gate with an accordion tucked under his arm. He introduced himself and explained at once that, like most his friends, he fully expected to be posted to the Foreign Ministry or some other senior government office. "I don't know how I ended up here," he said, casting a puzzled look at a sea of curious children. He was disparaging at first about his placement but, little by little, he grew to love the library. He even turned out to be a gifted storyteller and became very popular with the library members.

Michael stayed for two years and after he left, he later turned a room in his own home into a small library that he opened to neighbourhood children every Sunday.

KATHY LATER HIRED AND TRAINED ABIGAIL ELISHA, THE MOTHER OF two of the first members of her reading circle, to join Joanna as a permanent staff member at the new library. Abigail stepped easily into her new position and worked well with Joanna to help the library move ahead. Kathy paid them both a small salary, at first from her own savings and then from donations she was beginning to receive in Canada.

Joanna and Abigail were a perfect team to run the new library. It did not matter that neither of them had any education beyond a high school certificate; nor did they have any formal library experience. Kathy believed that, rather than hiring staff with a degree in Library Science, it was more important to recruit those with a warm and pleasant personality, who are hard-working, mindful of the importance of cleanliness, who love books and children and are committed to helping them learn to read in a friendly atmosphere. "Joanna and Abigail are excellent examples. They have both turned out to be perfect for the job."

After ironing out a seemingly endless string of last-minute details—ensuring a supply of soap and water for hand washing, purchasing writing and drawing supplies, ordering locally-made wooden puzzles—the new library held its official opening on November 13, 1992. Joanna marked the occasion by tacking up a signboard on the gate that read "Osu Library" with a quirky drawing of Curious George, the hero of the popular children's storybook, carrying a bright yellow library bag.

The Osu Library quickly became a popular fixture in the neighbourhood. One visitor who stopped by that first day said the new library looked like "a precious little dolls' house." Children swarmed in from all around to see what was inside this odd-looking building and they were thrilled with what they found. To Kathy's embarrassment, it was later decided to change the building's name to the Kathy Knowles Community Library, or KKCL, not only to honour its founder but to avoid confusing it with an older government library called the Osu Children's Library. However, for many who have a sentimental attachment to the original name, the building will always be called the Osu Library.

THE NEW LIBRARY OPENED FIVE AND A HALF DAYS A WEEK. FROM THE start, Kathy set the same high standards as before and expected everyone to respect them. She designated Monday as 'clean-up day' when the whole place is scrubbed down and all the books and puzzles are wiped clean. Cleanliness is a preoccupation of Kathy's, stemming perhaps from her nursing training. She seizes any chance to pick up a cloth and wipe down the dusty shelves. This is doubly important in Ghana, especially during the season of the Harmattan, the desert wind that sweeps down from the Sahara and carries with it a fine dust that seeps into every corner. Monday is also the day the staff cover all the new books with plastic. This too helps beat the dust and extends the life of the books.

Two wash basins, soap and a towel, lovingly embroidered with READ and a happy face by a Winnipeg volunteer, were placed on a wooden table at the entrance to the library so children could wash and dry their hands before they entered. Then they put their shoes on the shoe rack.

Once, when a senior government official arrived for a visit, he was taken aback when he too was asked to set an example and remove his shoes. He complied willingly.

After hands and shoes are dealt with, the children step into the library where they could choose a book from the shelf and read stories, fix wooden jigsaw puzzles, sing songs, or play educational games such as Scrabble or Checkers or *Oware*, a popular game in different parts of Africa.

Many of the children already knew the library rules but those who did not received careful instruction on how to care for the books. "We emphasized that before any child can take down a book, they must learn how to turn the pages without tearing them," Joanna explained, carefully lifting the top right hand corner of the page. "This is very important in a country where both the dust and humidity shorten the life of books." She has taught the children how to place the books back on the shelf, how to recognize a title or an author's name. Whenever possible, she pointed out to the children that books are very precious and that they are worthy of respect. Even the youngest ones who cannot read were offered a picture book and shown how to turn the pages. "This is the first step to reading."

From the start, Joanna also ensured that all the children using the library wrote letters of thanks which she sent to Canadian donors who had given money or books. "Thank you for building such a beautiful library for us," wrote Leticia, aged 12, in a carefully penned script. "You've given us the opportunity to read more books, to improve our speaking of English and to keep very serious with our work." Kuma, another library member, wrote: "I like the library because it is a peace place where you revise your mind." And from 13-year-old Portia, "We are going to do all that we can to make you proud by learning hard so that we can also be good citizens like you and do something better for our nation someday."

"We have always spent a lot of time writing these letters," Joanna says. "This way, the children learn that these books did not come from Kathy but from many friends 10,000 kilometres away."

AS THE NEW LIBRARY BEGAN TO TAKE SHAPE, KATHY FELT THAT SOME of the operating costs should be raised by the families of library members.

In November 1993, she and the staff organized their first sponsored walk, Terry Fox-style.

The week before the chosen day, the children dashed around the neighbourhood badgering family and friends to sign a pledge sheet and they managed to raise enough money to cover a small portion of the library expenses. On the big day, two children, one carrying the flag of Ghana and the other a flag of Canada, joined a lively brass band and led a parade of about 200 children and their families who ran or walked the eight kilometres from the library to the Accra Zoo and back. It was a joyful occasion, with everyone clapping and singing and waving banners and flags. The event has continued every year since, with destinations that have included a local TV station, the National Museum, a nearby fire station and the Kwame Nkrumah Mausoleum.

Some years later, when more space was needed in the library, Kathy added two smaller 12 foot metal containers to the original structure. One provided a small office for Joanna and another, a badly-needed space for storage. This time, the required permission to erect the two additions took only nine months. In 2009, she added another small container for the library's first computer lab to house seven donated computers. Library staff and volunteers are now guiding excited library members through the basic workings of computers.

WORD OF THE KATHY KNOWLES COMMUNITY LIBRARY SPREAD QUICKLY, not only around the neighbourhood but well beyond its borders. It wasn't long before teachers and would-be librarians from schools and villages around the country were contacting Joanna to seek help and advice about setting up libraries in their own communities. To meet the demand, Kathy and Joanna designed a two to three week training course which was offered free to lay librarians and teachers. Joanna leads these sessions and carefully steers the participants through the basics of setting up and running their own facility.

The idea was simple: those wishing to take part would travel to Accra to work with Joanna and learn from her all the details of running a library—how to handle, repair and cover the books; how to teach educational games; how to encourage various creative activities. In short, how to instil in children a respect for books and the love of reading. And always, she emphasized the importance of story time, something Kathy feels passionately about.

At the end of their course, participants receive a diploma before returning home with two boxes of books and a pledge to send Kathy regular reports on the progress of their own library. These initiatives could be as simple as reading stories to children under a tree, or it could be a room in a school, a church or a community centre. If progress is good, they receive additional help. If it is not, they are struck from the list. This outreach program continues to this day and has helped launch small and not-so-small libraries in more than 200 schools and communities across Ghana as well as lending support to library projects in Tanzania, Zimbabwe, Burkina Faso, Cameroon, Uganda, Mozambique and the Philippines. At least three of them carry the name "Kathy Knowles."

These training sessions proved to be very popular with more and more inquiries coming from inside Ghana and even from beyond its borders. In response to these requests, Kathy wrote a short booklet, *How to Set Up Community Libraries,* which contains such advice as how to conduct story time, what games to include, the selection and storing of books and the most suitable furniture for a children's library. Kathy acknowledges that she has learned much about setting up libraries and sees this small publication as a useful tool to help others do the same.

The Kathy Knowles Community Library has continued to grow in leaps and bounds. Two years after it opened, there were 700 active members who had made over 21,000 library visits that year. Their small stock of books quickly expanded to 4,000, thanks to donations from many Canadians and free transport provided by Canadian Airlines and Race Cargo Airlines during the 1990s. At the end of each month, Joanna continues to send a report to Kathy back in Canada noting any issues that arise as well as the all-important library attendance figures. "If the numbers are climbing and the library is well patronized, I know that things are going well and that we are on the right track," says Kathy. "However, if children aren't coming, I recognize that something is amiss. Libraries are still an unknown quantity in much of Africa and children need to be encouraged to enter, they need to be welcomed, they need to see a library as a fun place and reading as exciting. That is the challenge of a good librarian."

Visitors to the Osu Library are always impressed. When *Toronto Star* reporter Karen Palmer dropped by in 2006, she wrote: "What some people call 'the little blue library' is accomplishing something dozens of development groups, poverty fighters and non-governmental organizations are spending billions to do. It's giving African children a love of reading and an unlimited access to books—and all on a shoestring."

Holly McNally, former chairman and CEO of McNally Robinson, one of Canada's largest independent bookstores, was also in Ghana in 2006 and made a point of visiting the library. "This humble container has been transformed into a well-stocked library, a creative colourful haven and an oasis of joy," she wrote following her visit. "I arrived just before school was out on a hot weekday afternoon. Within minutes, the children arrived and kept arriving for over an hour. Some had walked long distances for the privilege of spending time in this happy place. They played games. They sang songs. They read books over and over again. This wonderful assemblage happens every day.

"Who could imagine that a 40 foot container, three librarians and a collection of books could bring such joy in learning and become an education for so many young children?"

KATHY HAD ALWAYS IMAGINED THAT, WHEN SHE WAS BACK IN CANADA, she would oversee the activities of the library through the regular reports she received from Joanna. It never occurred to her that she herself would ever return to Ghana. But two weeks before the family's departure in June 1993, when they were all immersed in last-minute packing, she attended a fundraising dinner at the US Embassy in Accra. The organizers were selling tickets for a raffle which included a return KLM ticket from Accra to Amsterdam. To her surprise—and delight—Kathy held the winning number! "That made me realize I was meant to return to Ghana."

John Knowles' posting finally ended in June 1993 and the time came for the family to leave Ghana. For Kathy, it was with very mixed feelings. "I didn't feel worried about the library," she said. "I knew that with Joanna in charge, all would be fine. But it was still hard leaving my baby behind." Others were not so sanguine. John recalls that many people—including himself—had very grave doubts that the library could function without Kathy's presence. "There were many people who feared that the place would fall to pieces once we left," he said.

As the day of departure drew closer, everyone in the Knowles family began to feel a deep sadness. Luckily, John and Kathy had retained their links with Canada. They had returned to their family cottage every summer and would soon be back in their own familiar house. This made the change easier, especially for the children.

Nevertheless, the day the family left their home in Ghana and headed for the airport, they were all in tears. "It was very emotional for all of us, for me, for the children, for John. We were all leaving something special behind." Many of their friends and their staff gathered on the airport roof to wave them goodbye.

Much later, Kathy spoke of the day when the family finally boarded the plane for home. "The day I left Ghana, I honestly thought the Osu Library was the ultimate goal for our organization. I thought this would be it. I never felt for a minute that it would go any further."

## CHAPTER 4

# Canadian Roots

WHEN THE FAMILY ARRIVED BACK IN CANADA, KATHY WAS HAPPY TO return to her Canadian roots where she had spent most of her short life. Though she had spent the previous four years immersed in library concerns, she had never been a teacher, nor had she received any formal library training and couldn't tell a Dewey Decimal System from any other method of library cataloguing. Kathy did acquire many useful skills as a youngster, but few were directly related to libraries.

She was born in Toronto on December 15, 1955 where her father, Gordon Lennard, worked as an executive with the Bank of Commerce. The family moved often, first to Ottawa then to Montreal and finally to Calgary where Gordon developed the first 'Flying Bank' in North America—an airborne banking service designed to help those living in remote northern communities. By the time Kathy reached five years of age, she had lived in five different houses.

Kathy was the eldest of six children. With every new addition to the family, she was expected to help with the younger siblings so she acquired a sense of responsibility early on. Even at five, she was changing diapers and giving bottles to each new baby that came along.

As if six children were not enough, the family also took in a Japanese music student who had come to Canada to study the violin. She fit in well with the family since music was an important pastime in their household and each child was encouraged to learn to play an instrument. Kathy opted for the viola when a friend told her that knowledge of this instrument would make it easier to realize a dream to get into an orchestra.

Her early viola lessons served her well. She was in high school when she won a spot in the 40 member Calgary Youth Orchestra and played with them for three years. A highlight was taking part in a European tour of England, Wales, Holland and Germany in 1972. To raise money for the tour, she sold hundreds of pounds of cheddar cheese and earned an extra allowance by doing all the family laundry. Music has remained an important part of her life. When she is in Canada, she and two friends try to meet every week to make music together in a loosely-organized string trio.

Kathy is the first to acknowledge that hers was a privileged life with parents who cared deeply about providing the best for their children. Most importantly, the senior Lennards made sure that their children were exposed to the world of books. Kathy still remembers all her early favourites, many of which still sit on a crowded bookshelf in her home office. *The Country Bunny and the Little Gold Shoe,* by Dubose Heyward was always a special choice, as were many of the classics, such as Frances Hodgson Burnett's *The Secret Garden* and *Charlotte's Web* by E.B. White. Books were also an important part of Christmas. Each year, her grandfather gave her a book and she still has many of those. Once it was *Chee-Chee and Keeko,* by Charles Thorson, a suspenseful story about how one act of kindness leads to another. Says Kathy, "That was the first time I really understood what the word 'kindness' meant."

Summers were special times for the family when the whole brood squeezed into their station wagon and headed north from Toronto to their grandparents' cottage in Honey Harbour. "It was wonderful up there, swimming and canoeing and breathing in Georgian Bay air," she recalled. "It was a timeless period we spent with both my grandparents whom I adored." One of her favourite cottage pastimes was collecting the laundry from the clothes line and carefully folding it into neat little piles. "I guess I'm what you might call a neatness freak."

GORDON AND BETH LENNARD FELT STRONGLY THAT TRAVEL SHOULD BE a part of their children's education, so each year they packed their kids into the station wagon and drove to some place of interest. They visited

Washington (the US Congress was a must) and Rochester (for a tour of the Kodak camera factory). There was a trip to Detroit (to visit the Ford Motor Company) and to Boston (to see Harvard University where Gordon had earned a graduate degree).

The most memorable summer trip was in 1971 when the family rented a Winnebago and drove almost 2,000 kilometres north from Calgary to Yellowknife, capital of the Northwest Territories. At Yellowknife, the family joined a Bank of Commerce officer on a DC-3 aircraft to accompany him on a tour to some of the remote northern Inuit communities. They flew up to the Arctic Circle and, each time they landed, a long line of people waited on the tarmac for the bank officer to help them with their banking needs such as issuing bank loans or making deposits.

That northern trip made a big impact on 16-year-old Kathy. It was her first exposure to the North and she would never forget the austere Arctic beauty and the warmth of the Inuit people. It was after visiting those communities that she decided she would like to work in the North. She quickly realized that the only way she could do that would be to train as a teacher or a nurse. That is when she decided on nursing. Her mother was not surprised by her decision. "There has always been a streak of service embedded in her somewhere," she said. "Even as a young girl, Kathy was always consumed with the idea of helping the needy. I remember when she was just nine, she stood on the street corner for hours selling tags for the Humane Society. Later on in high school, she wrote an aptitude test for a guidance counsellor and the results showed that she was so interested in service and helping others they suggested she would make a good nun!"

She chose to follow a nursing degree at Queen's University in Kingston, Ontario, and, in 1973, enrolled in the Nursing Science program. She was not a strong student and felt poorly prepared for the rigorous academic demands of the university but each year, her grades improved and she became more confident. "Maybe I spent too much time swimming." Indeed, competitive swimming had been a passion since Grade 7 so she easily made the Queen's swim team. She also won a place in the Queen's University orchestra.

Kathy received her Bachelor of Nursing Science in 1977. Upon graduation, she applied for different jobs, including several positions in the North and an organization supporting a leprosy colony in Africa. Most of the replies suggested that she needed to gain more experience. Finally, she learned of an opportunity to work in Moose Factory, a small native Cree community of 2,500 located in northern Ontario, more than 300 kilometres northeast of Cochrane, the nearest sizable town. Moose Factory was on an island and to reach it, you either had to fly in or take an overnight train to Moosonee and, in the summer, cross over by boat. In the winter, when temperatures could drop to minus 40 degrees, you crossed the frozen water by skidoo or boarded a helicopter. There was little more to the town than an Anglican Church, a Hudson's Bay store, a school, the hospital and a large native reserve.

Kathy signed up to work for a year as a paediatric nurse in the Moose Factory General Hospital which served the Inuit and Cree communities from both James and Hudson Bay. The ward she worked on dealt primarily with cases of meningitis, pneumonia and surgical emergencies. Tuberculosis was the major concern on the other wards. Few of the patients spoke English so Kathy tried to learn some phrases in Cree and Inuktitut but she usually needed to rely on an interpreter.

She faced many new experiences while serving in Moose Factory but one event stuck in her mind for years. She was nearing the end of her assignment when she was asked to fill in with another nurse on a Medevac mission, an air ambulance service which flies into distant villages to provide emergency medical care. She boarded the Medevac plane and flew to Port Harrison, a remote community now known as Inukjuak, to collect a small child who needed to be evacuated to the hospital. On the journey back, a woman who was also in the plane suddenly had a fatal heart attack so the two nurses placed her on the floor in the aisle and did everything possible to resuscitate her. Alas, sadly, they didn't succeed. The woman died before the plane touched down. That event hit Kathy hard. "I was devastated that we couldn't save that woman but we just didn't have the back-up help we needed. It was the first time a person had died in my care. I felt so badly."

Just weeks before Kathy was to leave Moose Factory, there was a strike at the hospital of some of the staff members. She was one of the few assigned to work during the strike but it turned out to be tough, chiefly because she wasn't familiar with the other wards. "I was desperately overworked and exhausted all the time so I finally decided I just couldn't continue."

Kathy left Moose Factory for Kingston. One important reason for choosing Kingston was the fact that she had become seriously interested in an old school friend called John Knowles who was finishing up a business course at Queen's. They had first met in the same Grade 6 class at Blythwood Public School in Toronto where they learned to square dance together during gym periods. The girls lined up on one side and the boys on the other. Then they chose their partners, and Kathy picked John.

The two went on to different high schools and after Grade 9, Kathy's father was transferred with his bank to Calgary. But during the summers, when John was at camp and Kathy at her grandmother's cottage on Georgian Bay, John recalls that they exchanged "streams of letters." Years later, they met up at Queen's, she as a nursing student and John in business. "She had a really full schedule, with her studies, her music and all her swimming events," John recalls. "And once, when I was invited to dinner, Kathy and her housemates all sat down and she put her head on the table and slept through the rest of the meal."

Although John claims he remembers few of his square-dancing skills, he does remember Kathy as "a quiet and soft-spoken person, certainly not a big party girl. We both enjoyed sports and a love of the outdoors. In fact, she could keep up with me in most sports and could easily ski down any hill I could."

However, their relationship was not always easy. Kathy remembers a period when she had serious doubts that it would work. She had been part of a women's Bible study group that was clearly important to her. John didn't share her strong Christian faith and some of her friends suggested that it would be hard to marry someone who didn't have the same beliefs. So she put the relationship on hold. After much soul-searching, she finally came to realize this was something they could work out. So they got together again and decided to marry when John finished the final year of his course.

The minute the school year ended, they moved to Toronto and were married on August 25, 1979. Kathy, then just 23, wore her grandmother's white silk wedding dress and carried a bouquet of gardenias, her grandmother's favourite flower.

The couple rented an apartment in a century-old house in downtown Toronto. John joined the accounting firm, Price Waterhouse Co. and Kathy worked in the Neonatal Intensive Care Unit of the Sick Children's Hospital. It was a challenging and often heart-wrenching job that occasionally involved caring for babies who were born healthy but with a heart defect that was not readily apparent at birth. Within a few hours after being born, it would become evident that the baby's heart was not compatible with life. "Everything would look so good at first but then they'd slip. There was a lot of heartache on that job."

AFTER THEY WERE MARRIED, KATHY AND JOHN INCLUDED SUMMER trips to his family cottage in Muskoka. It was during a visit there in the summer of 1986, just three weeks after Kathy had given birth to her third child, that the family was sitting on the dock and someone suddenly spotted a small plane flying dangerously low over the lake. Seconds later, there was an ear-splitting explosion as the plane nosedived into the water.

Despite her frail post-birth condition, Kathy jumped into a boat with three other family members and they raced to the scene. They found the pilot alive and conscious in the water after he had ejected from the plane but his passenger was trapped inside a flaming nearby boathouse where the plane had crashed. They shouted to the pilot to swim to their boat but he kept flailing his arms and crying out for help to save his passenger.

Kathy decided to act. She dove into the water, swam over to the pilot and quietly talked him into getting into their boat. He finally agreed and the others helped lift him in. Kathy winces at the memory of the whole event. "We were glad we could help save the pilot but one of my deepest regrets was that we weren't able to save his passenger. It was just not possible."

In typical modesty, Kathy brushes off her role in the rescue. However, the Royal Canadian Humane Association thought differently. They later presented her with a Bronze Medal for Bravery for her action.

ONE DAY IN 1986, KATHY AND JOHN WERE SCANNING THE NEWSPAPER and noticed an ad for a log house that was for sale. It was in Ospringe, a small hamlet close to the city of Guelph and an hour's drive west of Toronto. The next day, they drove out to have a look and immediately fell in love with the place. It was log cabin "with a lot of cracks in between" and heated only by a wood-burning stove. It came with 42 acres of land, a pond, a maple forest, and a Christmas tree farm. Kathy and John were both aware that this would mean a big life-style change and numerous challenges but they were ready to try country living. By this time, they had three small children, so they gathered up the kids, packed their bags and, just before Christmas 1986, they moved to their new home.

The change suited Kathy beautifully and the family came to love life in the country. They watched wolves and deer and other wild animals that roamed across their property. They tapped their trees for maple syrup and sold Christmas trees from their lot. Every corner of the property provided Kathy with a new outlet for her creative abilities. She built a stone wall and a meandering path to create a woodland garden with hostas, azaleas and beds of perennials. She spent many long hours working on her garden and savoured every minute of it.

Ospringe lay in a snow belt so the winters brought daily challenges. John and Kathy both learned how to drive a Massey Ferguson 35 horse power tractor to clear the snow from the half kilometre-long laneway from their house to the road. With three young children including a small baby, she had to drive everywhere. It was at least ten kilometres to the nearest doctor or to pick up a babysitter. And of course, driving was perilous in the winter on the icy roads.

Like many Canadians living in isolated communities, health issues were a concern since the closest hospital was miles away. Two of their children had a history of seizures and on occasion required emergency care. Schooling was another issue they had to face. Kaitlan walked to the end of the driveway to meet the school bus to a nearby town for kindergarten. Kathy drove Sophie to a Waldorf School for a nursery program half an hour away. She was impressed by the nurturing environment of the Waldorf School, a private pre-school with hands-on activities that involved artistic and creative play, such as singing and art. The highlight of every week was the day Kathy drove the whole family to a local library in Hillsburgh, a village ten kilometres away. "The children all loved that little library and Alastair always returned home with about 50 books! Happily, they all turned into avid readers."

During the time they lived in Ospringe, Kathy gave up her nursing work to be there for the children. She still found time to volunteer with a Rural Women's Support Program which offered help to abused women in the community. It was a seemingly idyllic life, a special time for making life-long friendships. Little did they know what lay ahead.

## CHAPTER 5

# Return to the Home Front

THE FAMILY RETURNED TO CANADA IN JUNE 1993 AFTER FOUR YEARS in Ghana. They moved back into their log house in Ospringe which had been rented while they were away, and John picked up various jobs as a consultant. It was a tough transition for them all since they had loved their time in Africa and Kathy, in particular, had developed close bonds with many Ghanaians. And of course, there was her little blue library. No matter how hard she tried, she could not stop thinking about how well it was functioning.

Kathy's top priority was to settle the children back into school and to care for Akos who was still at home. When their routine was firmly established, she set out to look for more second-hand storybooks for her library back in Ghana. Friends and nearby neighbours rallied to help her sift through garage sales and church bazaars and before long, she had collected, cleaned, sorted and packed hundreds of books.

She waited anxiously to receive Joanna's monthly reports. Communication with Ghana was challenging back then. The only reliable way to keep in touch with Joanna was by mail and letters took up to four weeks to arrive. Phoning was impossible since few people in Ghana had working phones.

Kathy breathed easier when Joanna's reassuring reports finally reached her. But as the year wore on, she found herself thinking how much she would like to see for herself how things were working out. She was still clutching her KLM ticket so decided, in early 1994, to use it to make her first trip back to Ghana. She would stay for just two weeks and, exercising the same monkish frugality that would continue to mark her every move, she welcomed an invitation to stay with friends.

When Kathy arrived in Ghana, she found that little had changed in Accra since she moved back to Canada. However, there were events outside Accra that were unnerving: in February 1994, the Northern Region of Ghana had dissolved into a tribal war, a conflict that left thousands of people dead and even more displaced. That same spring, even more disturbing news trickled in from much farther away: following an air crash on April 6 that killed the President of Rwanda, the country dissolved into warfare that sparked the murders of an estimated 800,000 people—20 percent of the population—that became the worst genocide in living memory. Even in distant Ghana, people were horrified by the events that unfolded.

KATHY'S FIRST STOP AFTER REACHING ACCRA WAS, OF COURSE, THE NEW library. Joanna welcomed her with a hug and she was delighted to find the place was running like clockwork. Children were turning up in large numbers and were sitting shoulder-to-shoulder on every available seat, all with their noses in books. Others were quietly fixing puzzles or playing board games. Within minutes of her arrival, Kathy pulled up a stool beside a group of children, plucked a book from the shelf and did what she enjoys more than anything else: she read them a story.

"*Once upon a time,*" she began. In Ghanaian tradition, the children replied "*time, time*" and the story continued. The children sat silent listening to every word. When Kathy finished the book, they clamoured for more. But there was work to do.

She then moved to a quiet corner and sat down with Joanna to discuss library details and to review her accounts. Joanna opened a large black ledger and Kathy checked each item carefully. "Library repairs go in this column, staff bonuses in this one," as Kathy pointed to different sections on the sheet. Kathy had taught Joanna to keep detailed accounts and, to this day, she carefully records all her expenses. As Kathy was leaving the library, she looked around at the children sitting quietly inside. "The children are so happy here," Joanna told her. "It is always a struggle to get them to leave!"

Then there was the job of sorting and storing all the books that were beginning to arrive from Canada. Joanna managed to squeeze some of the boxes into one corner of the library but with more books arriving later that year, they had to find a way to house them.

One evening, Kathy was invited to the home of Richard Beattie, a young Canadian working in Ghana as a CIDA (Canadian International Development Agency) officer. Richard had arrived in Ghana in September 1995 and had very soon heard about 'the container library lady.' "I remember Kathy looking around my house and asking in her winsome way, 'Richard, ummm, how many bedrooms do you have?' Before I knew it, I had turned my spare room into a book storage unit for the Osu Children's Library Fund."

IT WAS DURING THIS VISIT THAT KATHY LEARNED FROM JOANNA THAT the staff at Ringway Junior High School, a few blocks from the library, were interested in setting up a library in one of their classrooms and needed advice on how to proceed. Kathy stopped by the school and met with the teacher/librarians and showed them how to introduce stories as a way of promoting literacy. She also gave them a box of books as a starting point.

Before she left Ghana, she told them that if they sent her letters to Canada with positive feedback, she would arrange for them to receive more books. Reports from the school were encouraging so, over the years, the staff received more books. The project was so successful that eventually, the school was able to build its own free-standing library that continued to be well-used and well-run.

Kathy was pleased with the response from her visit to the school and especially by the positive reaction from the teachers. But foremost in her mind was the image of so many children swarming into the Osu Library. She could never have imagined that in one short year, the place would be running so smoothly and would attract so many children eager to enjoy the books and games. By the end of her two-week stay, she found herself wondering if she should be thinking about building another library. However, she could still remember the seemingly endless hurdles she faced constructing the container library—finding the land, securing the endless permissions, recruiting suitable librarians. If she were to build another library, where would she start? And how would she ever manage to raise the necessary funds?

On her return to Canada, the idea simmered for months. It had taken well over a year of very hard work to set up the Osu Library. The fact that she was now living thousands of miles from Ghana would make starting and finishing and monitoring such a project doubly difficult. Money was the most important consideration. If she was to undertake a new library, it would mean she would somehow have to raise the money herself.

Still undecided, she thought first she should take steps to improve the image of the Osu Children's Library Fund, the charity set up earlier by her mother. She first learned how to operate John's computer and set to work. A logo was a top priority so a family friend designed one showing a child reading an open book surrounded by the rays of an African sun. She then wrote a brochure describing the project and worked out a motto: "Sharing the Joy of Reading with an African Child."

But what next? She knew little about fundraising and had no idea how to begin. Since the Osu Children's Library Fund was registered as an official charity, donors could at least receive tax receipts for their gifts. That was a good beginning. But how could she convince Canadians to care about children half a world away who had no access to books, especially when the eyes of the world were focussed on the atrocities unfolding in Rwanda and Bosnia?

She began by writing letters, dozens of them, slowly tapping each one out on John's computer, addressing and signing them personally by hand. She wrote again to family members and friends and friends of theirs telling them about her dream to build another library. But it was tough going: she had been away from Canada for four years and was barely known beyond her own small circle of friends. "Furthermore," she added "I hated—just hated—asking people for money."

She tried approaching service clubs and church groups in her neighbourhood to help them understand her vision. A few helped and she welcomed their support. That December the family sold Christmas trees from their property with the proceeds supporting the project. As each day passed, she wondered if she would ever manage to raise enough money to build another library.

Just as she was about to give up, her fortunes changed. On Monday, July 10, 1995, an article in *The Globe and Mail* gave her the boost she so desperately needed. The headline read "A Tale of Two Libraries" and it was written by then staff writer and noted cartoonist Anthony Jenkins. In his piece, Jenkins compared his own richly endowed west-end Toronto library to Kathy's tiny library in Ghana. "In Toronto," he wrote, "my daughter can...choose from more than 16,000 books (excluding books-on-tape, records, films and videos) or, with a little help from her nine-year-old sister, she can surf the on-line catalogue, with access to well over half-a-million children's books in the Toronto system...Nose resting on the checkout counter, she has her choices for today, her own library card and her shoes on. In the Osu Library in Accra, she would not have that privilege..."

The article produced a flood of mail with letters arriving from every corner of Canada. Kathy was at John's family cottage in Muskoka when he called to say that letters and donations were pouring into the house. A steady stream of these were from readers who wanted to know how they could help. Many of them contained donations and Kathy acknowledged each one with a handwritten note. At last, as she tallied up the funds she had received, she realized that she could start thinking seriously about building another library.

Soon after the article appeared, Kathy was invited to speak at High Park Alternative School in Toronto which Jenkins' two daughters attended. The students' response was immediate: that year and every year since, they have run a giant used-book sale raising thousands of dollars for Kathy's libraries.

Tony Jenkins still remembers the day he visited Kathy in her country home, what he called "an open plan space surrounded by nature." On reflection years later, he recalled that what struck him most about Kathy was her 'ordinariness.' "She is not some Gandhi or Mandela or Mother Theresa," he said. "She's just an ordinary woman and mom without grandeur who had a simple idea and followed it up tirelessly as it blossomed—and seemed surprised by its success. She was someone we all could be but for that little spark that takes an ordinary person into the extraordinary and cannot be defined…Like most of us, and unlike Kathy," he continued, "I moved on and forgot about things. She didn't and that is what makes her great."

The avalanche of mail from the Jenkins' article made Kathy realize that her tiny operation run from a cluttered upstairs desk had forever changed. At long last, the OCLF bank balance looked rosier than ever before in its short life. Suddenly, the future looked full of possibilities.

AT THE SAME TIME THAT THE OSU CHILDREN'S LIBRARY FUND BEGAN to move forward, there were changes on the home front. In March 1996, John was offered a job in Winnipeg, a city a two and a half hour flight west of Toronto. It seemed perfect for him at this stage of his career and both he and Kathy felt it would be wise to accept the offer. "Winnipeg meant nothing to us," said Kathy. "We didn't know anyone there and the only real plus was that it was conveniently located halfway between John's parents in Toronto and mine in Calgary. We looked at it as another adventure and we've never regretted it. Now I feel very much at home here which is important when the rest of my life is somewhat fragmented." They were on the move again.

John set out first to start looking for a house while Kathy remained behind to allow the children to finish school and to pack up and sell the farmhouse. The children were sad to leave their country home and all their school friends but when they arrived in Winnipeg that August, they were excited to see their new house—a large three-storey building on Montrose Street that they quickly came to love. It was in River Heights, an attractive, older section of town with neatly mowed lawns stretching down to the roadside and lofty elms arching overhead.

Once again, Kathy had to find new schools for the children while she settled the house. She still found herself thinking about the small library she had left behind. Luckily, her two Ghanaian directors were able to pay regular visits to the library and they kept her fully informed. "Kathy has a great gift of giving people the means and encouragement to help themselves," says Florence Adjepong, one of her two Ghanaian board members. "That is why things worked so well, even though she was thousands of miles away."

Once the house and the children were settled, there was much to do. Kathy's new home quickly became a busy hub for everything relating to her fledgling charity. First, she set up a makeshift office in a corner of her bedroom. It was little more than a single desk, the top drawer of a filing cabinet and a second-hand computer. She had few computer skills but John helped steer her through the basics and she took it from there.

Top priority was finding more suitable, culturally-relevant books— books with images and faces familiar to African children. Once again, she visited garage sales and church bazaars and asked others to do the same. Word spread quickly and books began to tumble in. Some arrived by mail while more were dropped off on her doorstep.

KATHY HAD NEVER INTENDED TO EXPAND HER PROGRAM BEYOND THE one small library in the bright blue container. But she kept thinking about all the children swarming in to enjoy the storybooks. She had seen how they chose a favourite book and sat quietly, mouthing the words. She had seen how excited they were to learn to read and how that new-found skill helped nudge their school grades upwards. Then she would think about the thousands of children who did not have access to storybooks.

Now that the article in *The Globe and Mail* had provided such an enthusiastic and lucrative response, Kathy felt at last she could seriously begin to think about embarking on another library.

## CHAPTER 6

# A Library for Nima

THE IDEA OF BUILDING ANOTHER LIBRARY KEPT SWIRLING AROUND Kathy's head. She now had the funds to erect another building but where should she start? It didn't matter that she was 10,000 kilometres away from Ghana. She could at least do some of the spade work from her home in Canada.

She set to the job, using the uncertain phone lines to Ghana to begin another search for a piece of land. But there were plenty of frustrations. Phone communication with Africa ranged from interminably slow to impossible since landlines frequently broke down. Mail service was trying with letters taking up to four weeks to arrive.

She finally decided the only way to make any headway was to travel to Ghana, so she made ready to leave in the spring of 1996. Once again, it was a wrench for her to leave her young family. She also worried about the expense of another trip. But she had set her sights on this new library so, as before, she arranged for friends and neighbours to help John with the children and used her savings to purchase her ticket to Ghana.

Kathy could remember driving to school with her children along the Nima Highway in Accra, a busy street that cut through Nima, a sprawling and lively slum. Nima, together with its adjacent community of Maamobi, is one of the most deprived parts of the sprawling city. It is a densely populated shantytown of around 100,000 people who live jammed together under a sea of corrugated tin roofs. This is high-density living at its worst, with the most basic sanitation, limited water access and a wide gutter, awash with garbage and plastic, that slices through the area. Everywhere you look, children scramble along the dusty lane-ways, jumping over open sewers, cracked concrete or mounds of debris.

Mornings are the busiest time in Nima when the whole place is on the move—on foot, in battered trucks, on rickety bicycles or in ancient taxis. By first light, a steady stream of young and not-so-young women walk to the nearest water tap to fill their plastic buckets, prop them on their head and navigate their way back home through a labyrinth of narrow pathways. Home is usually a single room facing a communal courtyard shared by dozens of members of the extended family. That is where the women cook over a charcoal fire, wash and hang up their laundry, or gather to gossip.

In 2012, according to the CIA *World Factbook*, 68 percent of Ghana's population are Christians and just 15.9 percent are Muslims living mostly in the North of the country. The rest retain their animist beliefs. However, Nima is a predominantly Muslim community. They came down to Accra from the North of Ghana or from other nearby Muslim countries in the 1930s looking for work. Most of them found "temporary" digs in this corner of Accra and have never moved on.

When Kathy first arrived in Ghana, she had seen at once that people in Nima faced serious hardship. Many families were out of work and their children were not at school since their parents could not afford the school fees. The younger ones just hung about loitering in the laneways while the older ones, who also rarely found work, were often seduced by drugs or prostitution.

When Kathy was wondering about building a new library, she thought at once of Nima where the need was so great. The minute she arrived back in Ghana, she set to work. The phones were still unreliable so she covered the area by taxi or on foot to contact everyone she knew who might offer advice. She received dozens of tips but they led nowhere. Phone calls went unanswered. Whenever she mentioned the word 'Nima', people turned away at once, warning her not to go near the place. "Too dangerous," they would say, regaling her with stories about robberies, violence or drugs. She didn't seem to be getting anywhere. She returned to Canada disappointed but resolved to give it another chance.

By early the next year, in 1997, with the family installed in their new house in Winnipeg and the children happily settled in their new schools, Kathy felt she could travel to Ghana to renew her search for land for another library. An unexpected breakthrough triggered her decision to move.

A young Ghanaian man then living in Canada who had earlier bought a Christmas tree from the Knowles family at their farm in Ontario heard about Kathy's plan and claimed to be familiar with the Nima community. He told her to go to a place in Nima called 'Nima 411' and ask for a man called Mallam Mansuru who was an important figure in the community. That was just the encouragement she needed. She set out for Ghana determined to find him. After a long search, she finally managed to meet the man, a large and personable figure, who listened intently as Kathy explained her mission. He paused, thought for a few moments, then told her that the person she should see was Agnes Amoah, the assemblywoman (the local representative of the Accra Municipal Assembly) for Nima.

Kathy and Mallam Mansuru sought out Agnes in her home in the heart of Nima. She was a short, stocky woman who shuffled out of her room into the cluttered courtyard, welcomed Kathy warmly and gestured for her to sit down. Agnes's young grandson sat between them to translate Kathy's words into Fante, Agnes's language. Speaking slowly and pausing as the lad translated each sentence, Kathy shared her dream of building a library for the children of Nima and its neighbouring community of Maamobi. There was a long pause as her message was being digested.

The conversation continued. Kathy learned that Agnes had a small piece of land on the nearby Kanda Highway with an abandoned building on it. As she spoke, Agnes appeared to be interested in the idea of a library for the Nima children, even though she admitted she wasn't sure what a 'library' was. However, Kathy was not yet ready to make a decision so asked if she could think about it.

Kathy returned the next day. Another long discussion ensued. Finally, after a silent and thoughtful pause, Agnes finally said she would offer Kathy the land free of charge if she was prepared to renovate the building. She then signalled to Kathy to take her arm and cross the street to have a look.

Kathy couldn't believe what she saw. First of all, the small plot of land—barely half an acre—was just a few feet away from the busy highway with non-stop traffic roaring by, taxis jostling for passengers and street hawkers plying their wares. But it was the sight of the building that made her flinch. "It was a building of around 70 feet long and 20 feet wide but it was a complete wreck," she recalls. "The front part was missing a whole wall, the roof had caved in and the entire building was a shambles." Ted Gale, a Canadian civil servant who was visiting Ghana at the time, joined Kathy on that first visit. "There was a huge hole on one wall that looked as if a car had smashed right through it," he said, his eyes widening in amazement. "The roof was missing and the floor was covered with flattened cardboard where people had obviously been sleeping." They learned later that the building had been used as a haven for prostitutes and drug addicts. Furthermore, the land around it was completely bare, just hard and dusty sun-baked ground. There was not a blade of grass in sight.

Kathy's first reaction was to seek out another location. The constant traffic noise on the Kanda Highway would be a huge distraction for a library and, looking again at the building, she thought it would be impossible to do anything with it. She would have to restore a wall, replace the roof and so much more. "I wondered how I could ever turn it into a library or how I could improve the barren earth around the building." All night, her head was spinning as she tried to think of ways to salvage such a derelict structure.

She weighed the few pros and the many cons of the offer. She thought about the money it would take to restore the building and worried about its proximity to the highway. She thought about her own inexperience in building matters. They all seemed to be sending her warning signals. The next morning, it was as if she had had a revelation. She found Joanna and said to her, "You know, Joanna, I think I could make this work."

She returned to see Agnes the next day. It was late afternoon as she made her way along the narrow pathway into Agnes's compound just as the nearby muezzin began calling faithful Muslims to prayer. Agnes greeted Kathy with a smile and the two sat down together. There was another long discussion. "Are you still willing to donate the building for a library?" Kathy asked. Agnes smiled and nodded. "Then I accept your offer," said Kathy, reaching out to shake Agnes's hand. Kathy heaved an audible sigh of relief, bent over and gave Agnes a hug and whispered. "*Medaase*" ('thank you' in *Twi)*, the local language) and waved goodbye.

When Kathy shared the news with some of her friends, most of them were shocked by her decision. But she stood firm. "Everyone thought I was crazy to take on a project like this. This was a much bigger project than the Osu Library. Not only was the building in deplorable shape but, as my friends kept pointing out, Nima was notoriously dangerous with many well-known criminal activities. The city authorities called it an urban ghetto."

People also warned Kathy that security would be a big issue. Break-ins and robberies were widespread, for example. Others felt certain that anything she built would probably be wrecked within six months. "They were right to be concerned, but I had set my sights on helping this community. I knew I was taking a risk. I knew that security issues were there, that the place might be vandalized but I was willing to take that risk."

IN SPITE OF THE MISGIVINGS OF OTHERS, KATHY REMAINED DETER-mined to press ahead. First of all, she approached the Rotary Club of Accra who not only handed her a generous donation toward the reno-vations but arranged for a structural engineer to check if the building's foundation was structurally solid. She received a positive report. Then she began the lengthy ritual of visiting the Town and Country Planning Department to obtain the necessary building permissions. While she waited for their reply, she returned to Canada and launched an ambitious fundraising campaign for the estimated $34,000 she needed to rebuild the ruined structure. Again, she faced the burdensome task of asking people for money. But she was intent on restoring this building and she knew she couldn't do it without outside financial help.

Ted Gale, the Canadian friend who had visited the site earlier, answered her call and made a significant donation, along with his siblings, in memory of his parents. In doing so, he requested that their family name be included in the name of the library. Kathy consulted the community and they agreed that the new facility be called the Nima Maamobi Gale Community Library. These funds, together with those she had already received after *The Globe and Mail* article meant that she was ready to move.

Members of the Rotary Club began the process of restoring the building. They hired a contractor to supervise the installation of the all-important roof. If things went according to plan, Kathy expected that, by the time of her next visit, the building would be almost finished, she would then deal with any last-minute problems and arrange for the furnishings and books in time for the opening a week or two later. While she was in Canada, she hung onto every message she received from Ghana. Yes, things seemed to be moving along well, she was assured. Yes, yes, the library construction was on course and the project will be ready to open when you arrive.

AS PLANNED, KATHY RETURNED TO GHANA THE NEXT YEAR, IN MARCH 1998, together with her daughter Kaitlan, then 16. Early the next morning after arriving, they left for the site expecting to see the building almost completed. As her taxi drew up alongside the building, her heart sank. She couldn't believe what she saw. Things were far from finished. The place was basically still a construction site. She had thought from the reports she had received that the building would be finished and ready to open. "Well, it wasn't. One of the walls was still missing and the workmen still had a long way to go. I had long since learned that in Ghana, as in many other places, they tell you what you want to hear. But I guess I was naïve to believe all the glowing reports."

She was anxious to move things along as quickly as possible so she began at once to spend each full day on the site. The issues she faced were complex, to say the least. With the phones still unreliable, most enquiries for building materials had to be done in person which was not easy in a city filled with cars. Furthermore, there was no electrical source and all water had to be carried to the site. Since the contractor had obviously abandoned the job, Kathy took over the role. She had to rely on taxis to transport all the building materials including dozens of heavy bags of cement. She lost track of the number of trips she made to the far reaches of the city to purchase all the necessary materials.

Paying for the construction items as well as the salaries for her workmen posed another time-consuming hurdle. One hundred US dollars in Ghana's currency was then, in 1998, a cumbersone 231,000 Ghana cedis. She needed to change money often so on her visits to the bank, she carried a large over-the-shoulder purse, cashed her dollars, stuffed hundreds of well-thumbed cedi bills into her bag and surreptitiously climbed into a waiting taxi. For every payment she made to cover materials or salaries, she would dig into her bag, carefully count out a wad of bills, then hand them over. She then jotted down every cedi she spent, and, whenever possible, made certain to obtain a receipt for each item.

The project inched along, but progress was slow. Kathy knew she had to get things moving—and fast. She had booked to stay in Ghana for only a month so there wasn't a second to lose. She called the workmen together to discuss the situation. She had thought hard about a way to motivate them so offered free lunches to those who arrived on time, with their tools in hand and ready to work. Attendance improved dramatically.

But it was still a daily battle to move things along. "Unfortunately, I quickly learned that 'speed' and 'deadlines' and attention to details are not normally part of a Ghanaian's vocabulary. I learned a lot about patience on that project. But it was hard. The longer I spend in Ghana, the harder I try to be patient. But it isn't always easy for me."

Not surprisingly, unexpected glitches unfolded almost daily. As many of her friends had predicted, security was a big problem with thefts of materials happening regularly. One day, the electrician installed fluorescent security lights but those at the back of the library were stolen by the next morning. More seriously, as she tallied up her expenses, she realized she was quickly running out of funds. There were still materials to buy and workmen to pay so she dashed around the city asking for monetary donations or gifts in kind. A paint company gave her a generous discount on the paint she bought, and she received another discount from the company that made the plastic piping. Swissair gave a donation as did various women's groups—the Lebanese Women's Association, the North American Women's Association, the British Women's Association. Then a friend of Kathy's, Bubby Mohan, whose husband worked with Standard Chartered Bank, arranged for the bank to give a donation. Finally, at long last, she had enough money to finish the job.

Another offer of help followed. Old friends who knew she was relying on taxis to get around offered her the use of their car. "It was a kind offer but I was much too tired—and scared—to tackle the roads of Accra. So I passed on that one."

The whole thing dragged on much longer than Kathy had ever anticipated. Each day seemed to turn up even tougher problems. Just keeping the work going was a constant challenge. She decided to hold regular meetings with the labourers and painters, the plumbers and electricians—just to keep things moving. Even then, what she had expected to be done in a month stretched into three. "This really hit home when I received a dear little poem written by my daughter Akos, then only eight, saying how much she missed me. That struck me hard. But I knew I had to stay. I knew that if I returned to Canada, the project would never be completed. However, it was a great comfort having Kaitlan with me for part of that time." When Kaitlan left to return to Canada, Kathy recorded a taped message for all the children. This way, at least she felt she was connecting with her family.

Slowly, very slowly, the free lunches she gave the workmen began to pay off. The last wall rose, the tilers laid down a network of terra cotta floor tiles and Kathy's team of painters put the finishing touches on the building—pale yellow exterior with the wooden trim painted a vibrant blue. All the while, the citizens of Nima looked on with curiosity. They had never seen a building like this before and few of them had any idea what a 'library' was. They were amazed at the dramatic transformation of the once dilapidated building

When everything was nearing completion, Kathy contacted a local carpenter, Edward Modzakah, who was nicknamed 'Lufthansa' by some for his days working for the airline. She asked him to make nine child-size tables, shoe racks and shelves for the new library. She also ordered 80 small raffia-seated stools to be made by special needs youth at New Horizons School and hung colourful locally-made banners depicting African animals on the walls. Then she helped her mason, Bright Asare, lay a stone pathway that meandered from the gate to the front door using bricks left-over from the construction.

There was one important item left. Kathy hired a truck to haul several loads of black soil to the site and arranged for her workers to plant grass, trees and flowers around the library. She then ringed the property with bright pink bougainvillea shrubs.

THE FINAL WEEKS OF THE BUILDING PHASE WERE THE TOUGHEST KATHY had ever faced. She spent 12 hours a day, seven days a week, on the building site, supervising each step, checking every detail, noting every cedi that was spent, and constantly urging the workmen to keep moving ahead. As the days wore on, she became physically exhausted. She lost weight, had little appetite and was hardly sleeping at all. Emma Amoo-Gottfried became so concerned about Kathy's health that she sent her cook around every day with a hot lunch carefully wrapped in a colourful cloth and tucked into a wicker basket. "That was the turning point," says Kathy. "It made such a huge difference just to be properly nourished."

But it wasn't over yet. A young man named Seth turned up to help her plant the trees and shrubs in the garden and he worked hand-in-hand with Kathy for the last two weeks of the project. When she left for Canada, there were a few outstanding items still to buy so she gave Seth a list and some money to buy them. But he let her down. "He had built up this trust with me but he never followed through. That was a big disappointment. But it was a good lesson for me. I learned that there are very few people you can trust with money."

At long last, with only a few last-minute details left to complete, Kathy was relieved to see the workmen erect a sign at the gate of the building. It read 'Nima Maamobi Gale Community Library.' Opposite the sign, they planted two flagpoles. One carried the Canadian flag, the other the flag of Ghana. On windy days, the two flap side by side and still provide a colourful landmark on the Kanda Highway.

It was well over a year since Kathy had first set eyes on that dilapidated building. Now, as she stood before the Nima Library admiring the efforts of her workmen, she heaved a sigh of relief. It had been a long and excruciatingly slow process with many setbacks, but finally, the building was complete.

BEFORE THE LIBRARY OPENED, KATHY HAD TO DEAL WITH ANOTHER concern: finding a librarian to run it. After a long search, she was introduced to Hannah Agyeman who she felt at once would be a perfect choice. Like Joanna, Hannah had no formal library training, but she was a wise and gentle woman with a deep faith and a caring disposition. She was not only mother of three boys but she quickly became a much-loved mother-figure to half of Nima's children. She knew most of those who passed through the doors of her library.

An example of Hannah's confident handling of the most unexpected situations came in 2001 when she was chosen for a three-month placement in Canada as a volunteer with Canadian Crossroads International, a cross-cultural exchange program. It would be the first time she had visited Canada.

She set out from Accra according to plan and reached Amsterdam airport the next morning. It happened to be September 11, 2001, the day terrorists stormed the twin towers in New York. Planes on both sides of the Atlantic were immediately grounded so Hannah and thousands of other passengers spent the night in the airport waiting for news. The next morning, they were bussed into Amsterdam and taken to a Salvation Army shelter where they spent the next 48 hours. On the third day, some of them, including Hannah, were allowed to board a flight. "In the plane, everyone was very quiet. Then when we finally landed in Montreal, there was a burst of applause. I had goose bumps when I realized we had finally landed. I never imagined I would be so happy to reach Canada."

WITH HANNAH FIRMLY IN PLACE AS HEAD LIBRARIAN, KATHY HIRED five more staff members to help out. But before she could confirm their appointments, she had to firm up the question of payment of salaries and utilities. Kathy felt it was vitally important to obtain support from the Accra Municipal Assembly (A.M.A.), the local municipality, so even before she began building, she asked for their agreement in writing to pay staff salaries and water and electricity bills. This would not only mean a sharing of responsibility but, with staff firmly on the government payroll and the on-going payment of water and power guaranteed, it would help ensure that the project would continue.

"I had laid down only one condition with the A.M.A. before I started to build the Nima Library," she said. "I would build and maintain the building, supply the furniture and the books but I would not begin to build the library until the A.M.A. agreed to my request."

Although she managed to secure the signed agreement, actual payments didn't appear and the issue dragged on and on. Kathy wrote several letters and made dozens of phone calls and visits to the A.M.A. office in an effort to get them to act so the salaries could be paid. Florence Adjepong, her stalwart board member, was sympathetic. "Kathy is constantly meeting annoying officials who put up so much red tape and make it such a bureaucratic quagmire. Her perseverance, humility and soft-spoken nature do eventually win over even the most stubborn official. But it takes time and infinite patience. She is not one to give up. She pursues them in letters, in phone calls. She just wears them down until they finally give up." Kathy's old friend Richard Beattie who had seen her in action over the years gave her the nickname 'The Velvet Steamroller.'

It was almost a year before the staff members finally received their first pay cheque. In spite of that initial agreement, there continued to be a constant struggle to deal with unpaid water bills or interrupted staff salaries. It was a long and tough battle but at least an important precedent had been set.

THE NIMA MAAMOBI GALE LIBRARY OFFICIALLY OPENED ON JUNE 6, 1998. It had taken over a year and a half, two trips to Ghana and an abundance of patience to finish the project. And now, after the past three harrowing months, she was more than happy to join a glittering opening ceremony held outside the building. High-ranking officials dressed in their finery and tribal chiefs sporting colourful togas made of multi-coloured *Kente* cloth, Ghana's intricately woven fabric, joined many from the community who all shared in the excitement. There were speeches and songs and poems and dancing. As Kathy watched the children perform, the drudgery of the past months—the endless hours of fundraising, the frustrating negotiations with government officials, the hours she had spent on the site trying to keep things moving—all faded away. The event ended with a greeting from Kathy. As she returned to her chair, a friend stepped forward and presented her with a bouquet of flowers. "At that point, I was so exhausted, I just dissolved into tears. It was probably a culmination of many sleepless nights and all the stress of getting the project finished."

The celebrations ended and the guests passed through the doors to view the new library. Inside, they found a bright and sunny space with two rooms, one with tables for playing educational games such as Boggle and Bingo and solving wooden puzzles—elephants and lions and even a map of Africa are among the top choices—and a larger hall 40 feet long with round tables and stools for readers. More than 2,000 carefully-chosen books filled the shelves and 'kinder boxes' (box-like containers made suitably low for even the smallest children to reach) while colourful posters and banners made from recycled flour sacks covered the walls. Floor mats lay at the ready for the daily story time when all the children would gather inside, sit on the floor and listen to a story. The children quickly came to love those story times. In the Nima Library any day around 3.30 pm, the children start chanting "story time, story time!"

As the visitors strolled through the building, there was a real buzz of excitement. That night, Kathy collapsed into bed, exhausted but content. It was the first night in weeks that she had slept so well.

KATHY HAD ORIGINALLY PLANNED TO LEAVE FOR HOME RIGHT AFTER the opening. But since she had already invested so much time and energy in the project, she felt she should stay longer to make sure things ran smoothly. It turned out to be a wise move. On the first day the library opened, there were near riots when so many children tried to enter. Seth, the fellow who had been helping her, stood on a table at the gate handing out numbers for the children so they could queue up and wait their turn to enter. There were so many trying to get in that Kathy steered some of them off to a patch of grass about 100 metres from the library and read stories to them—just to remove some of the confusion from the front gate.

The crush of curious children continued so Hannah decided to run the library in shifts. Each child could spend just 30 minutes in the building but then had to leave to make way for others. Then they extended the time to one hour. "But it was very difficult," sighed Hannah. "They all wanted to come in at once."

Ten days after the opening, Kathy climbed on a plane for the journey home. She acknowledged that it had been the most difficult task she had ever undertaken but felt it was due to her own lack of experience. Although she was happy with the final outcome, the process had taken its toll. When she reached home, she stepped on the scales and found she had lost almost ten pounds.

## CHAPTER 7

# A Community Changed

KATHY ARRIVED HOME TO A WARM WELCOME AND A BOUQUET OF flowers from John and the family. This had been her longest and toughest visit, especially when she had had to extend her stay in Ghana to three months. She knew her absences were hard on the family, especially on her teenage children who were often hurt by their mother's divided loyalties. But Kaitlan, the eldest, shrugs off any feelings of resentment. "While she was away, sure it bothered us but we got used to it. Mom usually hired someone, a surrogate somebody, to stay and cook meals and care for the younger children so at least we all ate well and the laundry was done." Adds John: "Before she arrived home, we would all rush around cleaning the house from top to bottom. Then she'd come back and clean it all again! She's an obsessive cleaner."

Partly to assuage some of the guilt she feels about spending so much time away from home but also to help her children realize the importance of her mission to bring books and reading to disadvantaged children, Kathy has always tried to involve them in whatever she is doing. One way she and John have agreed on is to give each child the chance, when they reach 16 years of age, to travel to Ghana as a sort of 'rite of passage.' The children would work at after-school jobs to raise half the fare and Mom and Dad would cover the rest. Over the years, since the family returned to Canada, all four children have made their first trip to Ghana and now, more than a decade later, are returning for a second time. In 2011, Kaitlan made her third trip to Ghana, this time with her husband and baby daughter, Ginny.

On each trip, the Knowles children have undertaken some sort of project. Alastair travelled the country demonstrating a peanut-shelling machine that he hoped would save villagers hours of labour and contribute to library coffers. Kaitlan, who followed in her mother's footsteps by training as a nurse, used her expertise by assembling small first-aid kits and gave them out, together with detailed instructions, to all the library staff. Sophie is a graduate in music and in November 2009, she directed a lively musical opera called *The Orphans of Qumbu* that played to full houses for three performances.

John Knowles has also done more than his share to support the project. "When I married Kathy, I knew she had a big spark of life in her. But I wasn't certain how much initiative or confidence she had," he said. "Over the last 20 years, all that has changed and this has become a real mission for her. I am more than happy to cheer her on from the sidelines." However, he admits that he does often worry about her safety on these trips. "I worry most when she travels in some of those taxis where you can see through the floorboards." He is now relieved to know that she uses the same reliable taxi and driver.

Kathy's family and friends marvel at John's quiet endurance which they consider almost as heroic as Kathy's work overseas. "How many men would agree to let the mother of their children be away for such long stretches of time?" asked one of her friends. "He supports it, because he believes so strongly in Kathy's work. He is much more than 'the guy who helps lug the books down to the basement.' He is a calm and reassuring presence, both when she is at home and when she is away."

John has visited Ghana twice since returning to Canada and he keeps a close eye on developments with the project. "John loves Africa as much as I do and he is very much at home in Nima," says Kathy. "He has helped with the literacy classes there, worked with my dear carpenter and, by doing so, I think he has seen that all my efforts to raise funds in Canada have paid off."

John, in his own quiet way, is probably Kathy's strongest supporter. As he sits sipping coffee in his Winnipeg kitchen during a rare moment of calm, he shares his thoughts about the woman he married. "I guess we enjoy the same sense of adventure, though she has taken her's to much loftier heights! I marvel at how she has blossomed over the years and has become so confident at running this growing organization. But then, I am not too surprised. She identified a real need and she has done an amazing job in helping to meet it. I firmly believe that Kathy's involvement with the library has helped bring out many of her attributes such as her management and leadership skills." He pauses to attend to another visitor stopping to drop off books on their front doorstep.

"Kathy believes so strongly that there is a huge untapped potential among those kids and that giving them this exposure to books helps unlock that potential. She knows that if these children don't get a break, they could end up spending their lives scratching out an existence, or just getting into trouble. There are so many examples of the way in which our books have triggered a spark that sets a child in the right direction, that has become a flame of learning and that has meant better health, better grades, a better job and who knows what else. That makes it all so worthwhile and it is undoubtedly what keeps her going."

BACK IN CANADA, KATHY WAITED EAGERLY FOR NEWS OF THE NEW NIMA Library and was never happier than when Hannah reported that not only were the children flocking to the library in record numbers—6,000 members registered in the first month alone—but that the place had already begun to bring about change in the Nima community.

Abdul Moro Taufic, a young man in his 20s who would later head up another of Kathy's projects, grew up in Nima and is more familiar than most with the mood of the community. He was blessed with parents who sacrificed much to send him to school. He then managed to complete a degree in social work at the University of Ghana and worked in the Nima Library as part of his National Service requirement. Taufic, more than anyone, has been a witness to the changes the library has brought to the community.

Standing outside the library, neatly clad in an immaculate white shirt and dark trousers, Taufic speaks with a sense of wonder at the presence of the library in his community. "The first day I stepped into this building, I said 'Wow!' What a great opportunity for the children in Nima. I thought how lucky those kids are. They have something we never had." He pauses to greet a handful of children skipping along the pathway to the library. "Many of these kids were living on the streets before this place was built, but look at them today! When I watch them coming out of the new library, I can see so much excitement in their eyes.

"And just as important is the fact that the library is not only helping children learn to read but it is making people in this community much more aware of the benefits of education. It is making them realize that if their kids are ever going to move ahead, if they are ever going to break the cycle of poverty, they need to learn how to read. That is a big step forward."

KATHY RETURNED TO GHANA IN 1999, A YEAR AFTER THE OPENING OF the Nima Library and the morning after her flight, she headed straight to the new facility. No one knew she was coming so she tiptoed through the front door, chucked off her shoes and stepped inside. To her delight, she found the room packed with children. Most of them were sitting quietly at small tables reading. One group squatted on floor mats playing with building blocks while others sat at a table working on puzzles. The place was quiet and orderly and it was also clean and tidy. The garden was flourishing and the bougainvillea shrubs were already bursting into brilliant shades of pink and orange. "For me, the satisfaction comes from seeing those children looking so happy," said Kathy in reflection. "I feel that the poorest of the poor just aren't noticed. But here in the library, they are welcomed, they are respected and they are noticed. It is the staff who deserve the credit for this."

Looking back, Kathy is the first to acknowledge that, to start a library in a new area, especially one as deprived as Nima, was certainly a huge risk. She was always aware of the hazards but her determination to help the kids in this community kept her going. She also recognized that there were always skeptics around her. "One person cautioned me that, if I returned in six months' time, I was certain to be disappointed. It was a rough area and they felt that the money invested in this project would never pay off. I can understand their concern."

In her talks with Hannah, she learned that at first there had been much aggression among the children and they were noisy and undisciplined.

But Hannah and her staff established a strict routine and laid out rules. They concentrated on helping the children learn that, in the library, they must not fight, they must be polite and quiet and they must respect the building and the books. "Whenever they misbehaved, I told them to leave the library and not return for three days," said Hannah. "Then I could see them standing outside the gate, sobbing, sobbing. After three days, they would appear sheepishly at my door and say 'Madam, I have come.' That usually did it." It was a slow process but, little by little, the children began to obey the rules and to show respect for their new library.

Hannah's gentle but firm hand has had the effect of calming the most unruly children. She spends much of her time and energy getting to know each child, meeting their families, counselling them when necessary. "The library soon became more than a place for the children to read books and do puzzles," said Hannah. "For many of those kids, the library became their home."

In 2013, the Nima Library is just as popular as it was when it opened 15 years ago and it still sparkles with Kathy's spirit and ingenuity. More and more books fill the shelves and kinderboxes. The wooden jigsaw puzzles, once brought from Canada but now all locally made, are placed on open shelves for easy selection. Educational games are stored in a corner cupboard.

The staff members all look smart in uniforms made from batik cloth hand-dyed by one of the former literacy students. Dark letters on a turquoise background spell 'Joy of Reading' surrounded by the adinkra symbol known as *matemasie* meaning wisdom and knowledge. These are characters traditionally printed on Ghanaian cloth and representing proverbs, objects or animals.

The trees and shrubs around the library are now a lush contrast to the dusty playing field it borders. A grassy lawn covers the front entranceway, and a mound of plants including a spray of papyrus is growing apace. Kathy has always felt that for children who don't have much beauty in their lives, it is important to make her libraries as attractive as possible. As a nod to Canada, discretely nestled among the flowering plants is a small stone Inuksuk, a pillar of carefully balanced stones like those that serve as signposts for travellers in Canada's North.

Helen List, an Australian woman who came to Ghana in 1993 and now runs the highly successful Afia Beach Hotel in downtown Accra, has watched the evolution of Kathy's libraries from the start. "For these children to come into such a beautiful environment, with flowers and grass and trees and, of course, all the high-quality books is mind-boggling. What is even more amazing is the fact that the library is still as clean and tidy as the day it opened. That is no small feat in a country such as this."

SINCE ITS BIRTH IN 1998, THE NIMA LIBRARY HAS NOT ONLY INTRO-duced thousands of children to books and reading but it has developed in many other directions. Some initiatives were successful and others short-lived but Kathy felt each one was worth trying. A savings and credit group encouraged women to raise funds to launch small trading businesses. They deposited the equivalent of 11 cents a week and at year's end, Kathy and an anonymous donor matched their savings. In the early days, Hannah held 'Friday children's classes' to give eight needy children who were not at school a chance to learn. These lasted more than three years.

At different times, the library has hosted a stamp club and a wildlife club. There has been an enthusiastic drumming group, a dance troupe and a Joy of Reading choir. A bathing program offered children from deprived homes a towel, a bucket of water and soap for washing up. A teacher of people with hearing problems taught the children sign language which Kathy saw as a means of creating an understanding of those with disabilities.

In 2006, a dozen eager readers in their early teens met to form a book club, a new idea for them. They chose the books they would read and started off their first meeting with a lively discussion of the novel *Things Fall Apart* by the late African writer Chinua Achebe. *The Joys of Motherhood* followed, about the role of women in society by the Nigerian writer Buchi Emecheta. And Kenyan author Ngogi wa Thiongo's *Weep Not Child,* a book that examines the relationship between blacks and whites prior to that country's independence, was another popular choice. "Those meetings were fantastic," enthused Martin Adjei Legend, one of the first teenage members. "This was the first time any of us had ever actually discussed books and it was such a huge revelation for us."

One of Kathy's earliest volunteers brought another new idea to the Nima Library during a visit in 1999. Faith Avis, then a spry 75-year-old Canadian journalist, spent many hours of her stay reading to the children and helping out where she could. On most mornings, she was startled to see many of them with their heads on the tables sound asleep and she asked Hannah why. "They have probably come here without any breakfast," Hannah told her.

Faith couldn't get the sight of those children out of her mind. So she decided, with Kathy's permission, to set up "Faith's Food Fund" and each month after her return to Canada, she would send Kathy money to cover a hot lunch for 20 or more of the most needy kids. Every day at noon, a string of youngsters sits patiently on the bench outside the library waiting for what could be their only meal of the day. "I was so glad I could do something to help those kids," said Faith. "As I watched Kathy on the go from 6 a.m. till midnight, day after day, I thought that this was the least I could do." Faith supported the program until her death in 2010. Happily, a friend of Faith's stepped in to make sure the program would continue.

IT WAS NOT LONG AFTER THE OPENING OF THE NIMA LIBRARY THAT Kathy became aware that there were many bright children in the library who were not attending school since their parents were unable to pay the school fees. By western standards, the fees at the primary levels were small—only about $20 a year. But families still had to pay for their children's uniform and shoes, a school bag and notebooks which could amount to another $25, a hefty sum for parents who were often earning so little.

Kathy had received a donation from a family member to honour her late grandmother, Mimi, and she decided to use the money to set up a fund to enable a few of the most deserving children to attend school. She called it "Mimi's Scholarship Fund".

At first, she gave scholarships only to primary school children, but after 2005 when the government began to provide primary schooling for free, she was able to help a few of the most deserving students finish high school. Since fees at the high school level quickly rocketed upwards bringing the cost to between $500 and $550 per student per year, it is easy to see why many students had to drop out when they reached high school.

Choosing those who deserved a scholarship from the many who needed help always posed a challenge. Kathy relied heavily on Hannah who knew the background of most of the children who came to her library, so she was able to identify the ones with the greatest need.

One of the first recipients was Joshua Atimbila, a bright lad whose father died when he was young, and his single mother never managed to earn enough to pay his school fees so he had to drop out of school. Hannah noticed that Joshua hung around the library day after day reading most of the books on the shelves. She became concerned that he wasn't in school since he was clearly a clever boy. She suggested to Kathy that he receive the first scholarship and this allowed him to finish primary school. He did so well that Kathy continued his scholarship through high school which he completed with good marks. He continued to visit the library most days and, by the time he was 16, he was able to discuss all his favourite authors—Charles Dickens topped his list—with anyone who would listen.

When Joshua finished school in 2007, he joined the staff of the Nima Library and helped out for two years. He is an energetic young man who has already demonstrated considerable acting talent so he has chosen to study film and theatre.

Another scholarship recipient was Pius Benia, a serious young man who received a scholarship through to high school with excellent marks. In September 2011, he won a place at the University of Ghana where he studied Biological Science. On Kathy's most recent visit to Ghana, Pius greeted her with the exciting news that he had just received a full scholarship from the University to enter the newly-opened School of Veterinary Medicine, the first vet school in the country.

Talata Abomoi was another early scholarship winner. She is a lively young woman with a broad smile and a surprisingly rosy disposition, given her background. She had grown up in the North, in an unsettled family situation. Her father had died when she was two, but since he had never paid the customary 'bride price,' the family had to move out of their home. Talata's mother and her three small children lived on the street, working and sleeping in the market stalls. Her younger brother died of malaria or starvation ("we never knew which") before he was a year old so her mother sent Talata, then barely five, to live with her grandmother. "That was a nightmare for me," recalls Talata, wincing at the memory. "My grandmother made me work all the time. I had to do the cleaning, the cooking, the shopping, fetching the water. When all that was done, I had to take the cows and sheep out to the fields."

School was out of the question, undoubtedly because education for girls is a low priority for most families. "I wanted to go to school so badly," she said. "Every day, I prayed that somehow, I would have the chance."

Talata was six when her mother remarried and travelled with her to Accra. Talata and the couple and her step-brother all shared one small room with no electricity, no indoor toilet, no running water. One of her jobs early each morning was to walk to the far end of the compound and fetch enough water for the family's cooking and washing needs. This often meant two or three trips, each time returning home along a narrow and undulating pathway while she balanced a heavy bucket of water on her head.

The atmosphere in her home was grim with her mother and step-father fighting constantly. "They were always quarrelling and whenever I asked my stepfather about going to school, he would say 'Go to your mother' and I would go to her and she would say 'Go to your father'." By then, Talata's mother was selling rice and sugar in the market so she finally agreed to pay her daughter's school fees. But the support was short-lived. After only a year, Talata had to drop out of school because the fees were not paid. She was not yet seven years old.

One day, a friend told Talata about the newly-opened Nima Library. "I was so happy to find that place," she says. "I remember going into the library for the first time and there were so many books. I thought 'Wow. Where do I start?' I went nearly every day and I taught myself how to read. Then I would make a big pile of all the books I wanted to read and I would stay there until I finished them all. I just loved sitting in that beautiful place surrounded by books."

Talata was leaving the library one afternoon when she saw 'this beautiful white lady' entering the building. "I heard that her name was Aunty Kathy. I had never seen a white person before and I was so frightened, I ran away." Hannah had come to know about Talata's situation and asked Kathy if she could be helped by the scholarship fund. Kathy agreed that she would be a worthy recipient. "When I heard that, I just couldn't believe my ears," Talata says, her eyes popping at the memory. "The next morning, Hannah gave me a school uniform, new shoes, a school bag and books. I was off to school."

Talata was still expected to do much of the housework which meant rising very early to do her homework by flickering candlelight before setting out at 5 a.m. to fetch the water for the family. Nonetheless, she worked hard at school and at the end of that first year, she neared the top of every class. She continued to receive good marks so Kathy paid her school fees for the rest of primary school. Based on those results, she continued her support until Talata completed her high school courses in June 2007, again with top grades.

Talata has now set her sights on entering the University of Ghana. Knowing that her family could not afford even the modest university fees, she is working long shifts as a waitress in order to save for her university expenses. She has also helped teach evening adult literacy classes four nights a week and has turned out to be a gifted teacher. "Teaching comes quite naturally to her," says Kathy. "Because she's been through such hardships herself, she can identify with the adult literacy students who haven't had the privileges she's had. She made all her classes fun, each one peppered with quizzes and spelling bees. I am so proud that someone we have helped is now giving back in such a meaningful way."

Talata has grown into a confident young woman with a thoughtful, measured manner. Surprisingly, after a life of so much struggle and poverty, she bears no bitterness, has seldom asked for money, even though her needs are vast. In fact, she used a sizable chunk of her first year's pay to cover her mother's bills when she was hospitalized with serious stomach pains.

Sitting on a bench outside the Nima Library, Talata speaks of her lifelong dream of becoming a doctor. "I want to help people and this is one of the best ways," she says earnestly. "After that, I would like to specialize in gynaecology." Why gynaecology? "When I took my mother to hospital, I saw how badly they treat women patients. I would like to do everything I can to change that."

NOT ALL THE OCLF SCHOLARSHIP STUDENTS HAVE MANAGED TO FIND work after finishing school. Jobs are scarce in the best of times and students from Nima, in particular, face serious discrimination when looking for work. Other scholarship students who, though promising, barely had a chance to develop a career. One was Rukaya Ibrahim, a stunningly beautiful young woman who lived in Nima. Her father had died and her mother was seriously ill so she could never finish school. She did, however, show a strong artistic talent so Hannah arranged for her to follow a six months' course in batik and tie and dye. She finished the course and set up a workshop in the room she shared with her mother. She quickly attracted many clients and built up a small but successful business. In fact, her work was of such high quality that Kathy asked her to dye the fabric to provide new uniforms for all the library staff.

Soon after her mother died, Rukaya, married and learned she was pregnant within the first year. It was after four or five months that she began to feel tired and in considerable pain. When she started bleeding, she visited a nearby hospital and learned that her baby was lying outside the womb—called an ectopic pregnancy—a condition that is life-threatening for both the mother and the baby. She was advised to move to a bigger hospital with better equipment but she never made it.

Joanna was one of the first to hear the news. She called Kathy in Canada and, choking back tears, she whispered into the phone "Rukaya is no more." Both the mother and her baby had died in the hospital.

It is a sad fact that, in Ghana, as in much of Africa, infant mortality is still a grim reality stemming largely from lack of education, inadequate medical care, and hospitals that are understaffed and badly equipped. According to the CIA *World Factbook*, Ghana's infant mortality rate in 2005 was 51.5 deaths per 1,000 live births. That figure has dropped only slightly and by 2012, it showed 47.26 deaths per 1,000 live births. Maternal mortality also remains a serious concern. UNICEF cites that, in sub Saharan Africa, a distressingly high one out of 16 pregnant women will die before or while giving birth.

SO FAR, OCLF HAS MANAGED TO FUND SCHOLARSHIPS FOR MORE THAN 100 students. At first, only the neediest library members received them. Now, Kathy is imposing stricter guidelines. Students must have received a minimum grade of 20, the North American equivalent of a B grade, on their B.E.C.E. (Basic Education Certificate Examination) exams taken at the conclusion of Grade 9 to be considered for a scholarship. She also expects all scholarship students to put in four hours a week helping at one of the libraries. If they fail to do so, they are struck from the list.

Kathy often encounters other children who simply need a helping hand. In 2002, she was waiting for a taxi on a busy street corner when a young woman of about 13 asked Kathy if she knew where she could find work. Her name was Seraphine Danso and she explained that she had no parents and her grandfather had sent her down from the Volta Region to find work. She had just 2,000 cedis (25 cents) in her pocket.

Kathy talked to her for a long time to better understand her situation as it was hard to believe that such a young girl would be sent to the busy capital without support. She was afraid if she left her there on the street without any money, she might turn to prostitution so she took her to a shelter for teenage mothers, the only place she knew. She left her a little money and suggested she visit Hannah at her library.

Eventually, a social worker found Seraphine a place to live with other young women. Kathy gave her a scholarship so she could return to school and she managed to finish high school with good marks. At school, she also turned out to be a top runner and she wrote to tell Kathy she was entering a big sports competition but she didn't have any shoes for the race. So Kathy bought Seraphine her first pair of running shoes.

It happened that Kathy's next visit coincided with the big competition so she stopped by the stadium arriving just as Seraphine was about to run. After the event, an announcement came over the loud speaker that the winner of the race was Seraphine *Knowles*! Seraphine has kept her chosen name, is now managing well on her own but she has never forgotten Kathy's timely intervention when she needed it most. "Kathy has given new hope to so many youngsters," says Emma Amoo-Gottfried: "Especially through her scholarship program, she has given these kids, particularly the girls, the confidence that they can do anything. Now they can say 'My future is in my hands. I can further my education. I can choose my husband. I can have a say in what I want to become.'"

FROM THE DAY IT OPENED, DEMAND ON THE NIMA LIBRARY AND ITS hard-working staff continued to grow. The number of members expanded every year and, on some days, as many as 150 children jostled for a spot to read. "I wish everyone could see inside that library," says Kathy. "It speaks volumes about what is possible with limited space and a relatively small budget. And what is really neat is that, on any given day, there are Muslim children (the girls recognizable by their white head scarves) sitting and reading shoulder-to-shoulder beside their Christian friends, all in perfect harmony. They read together, they play together, they celebrate each other's festivals." The same harmony exists among Muslim and Christian adults in Nima. They begin and end every meeting and workshop with a prayer for Christians and another for Muslims. The government too observes national holidays of both faiths. "It is such a good lesson for the world."

Several of the earliest members of the Nima Library have now 'graduated' and are returning to help out. "It is so satisfying to see the children who passed through our libraries coming back to help," says Kathy. "Joshua and Talata are both excellent examples but, each year, there are others coming along. My hope is that among these graduates, there might be some who will eventually become permanent staff members at one of our libraries. After all," she adds, "it's not all the big stuff, such as the building, that is the most important. It is the individual lives we've managed to touch."

Emma Amoo-Gottfried lives less than a kilometre from the Nima Library and, over the years, has observed Kathy's libraries develop, especially the one in Nima. "What happens in that library is nothing short of phenomenal," she told me, standing outside the building as packs of youngsters swarm past her. "Everyone had given up on most of those kids. But Kathy has taken them off the streets and shown them something more. She has transformed their lives. Indeed, the minute those kids enter that library, a whole new world opens up for them. It is amazing what happens in that place."

## CHAPTER 8

# The Gift of Literacy

ILLITERACY, TOGETHER WITH THE CURSE OF POVERTY AND DISEASE, continues to plague much of the African continent. Ghana is no exception. A United Nations Development Program report shows that in 2011, the literacy rate in Ghana was 72 percent for men with a lower rate of 60 percent for women. And in the North, fewer than 10 percent of women can read or write. This wide discrepancy exists because women are born and bred to look after their children, to do the shopping, the cooking—all the duties needed to provide for the family. They are also brought up to respect and serve their husband and male relatives. All this leaves precious little time for schooling.

There is no doubt that the crux of the problem stems also from the school system which, in Ghana, has been in a dismal state for decades. Teachers are overworked and dispirited. Classrooms are so overcrowded that children have to triple up on wobbly benches. Many classrooms lack enough desks while textbooks and writing materials are woefully inadequate. In such crowded situations, it is not surprising that discipline is often a problem with frustrated teachers resorting to 'caning' (beating with a stick) when a child misbehaves.

Unfortunate also is the fact that there is not a single ounce of creativity built into the school day. Even if teachers had the time or the inclination to encourage creative activities, such as writing stories or poems or drawing, they haven't got the materials. Furthermore, school buildings are crumbling from overuse and disrepair: as recently as 2005, only 58 percent of Ghanaian public primary schools had toilets and even fewer, just 47 percent, had drinking water.

Most serious of all is the fact that, according to a UNICEF report published in 2003, a persistent 40 percent of children at primary school level (between the ages of six and 11 years) simply did not attend school. This improved slightly with the introduction of food programs in many schools. The reasons are easy to understand. Until 2005, it all came down to the fact that the obligatory school fees were, for many parents, simply beyond their reach. This meant that thousands of children stayed home or roamed the streets, robbed of the chance to learn to read and write.

However, there was hope on the horizon. In 2002, all 191 member states of the United Nations signed the UN Millennium Declaration which included eight millennium development goals. A pledge to eradicate hunger and poverty by 2015 topped the list. The second goal was the achievement of universal and free primary education by the same year. Ghana, to its credit, finally addressed the problem and in 2005, the government announced an end to school fees at the primary level. The country exploded with joy. At long last, children could attend primary school for free.

Well, not exactly for free. The family was still expected to provide all the extras—the uniform, a back pack and shoes, for example. Other expenses, too, began to creep in, such as parent-teacher association dues, fees for registration, fees for exercise books and fees to write exams. After-school classes suddenly sprang up for yet another fee. The policy of the Ghana Education Service does not condone extra classes but this generates added income for the teachers so the pressure is there. Despite everything, it was at least a start.

A little more than a month after the announcement of free primary education, more than a million Ghanaian children who had never been to school turned up to register. Enrolment suddenly jumped from a previous 5.9 million children to 7.2 million.

Many people applauded this long-overdue initiative. However, there were unfortunate side effects to the lifting of school fees for primary schoolchildren. Granted, more children were attending school, but the facilities and the teachers were barely able to cope with the sudden influx. Funds had not been allocated to build more schools, nor were there funds available to hire more teachers. The result was that, almost overnight, school rooms became even more overcrowded with as many as 80 children, sometimes up to 100, crammed behind desks intended for half that number.

Even more serious was the huge pressure placed on teachers. The pace of training new teachers increased but did not come close to meeting the demand. One observer, who attended a Ministry of Education meeting in 2011, told me that the country was then short 28,000 teachers! A quick band-aid solution was to use untrained and volunteer teachers to help out. Not surprisingly, those already teaching became dejected and unable or unwilling to cope. Sure, there were more children sitting in classrooms, but they were hardly learning anything substantial.

Sitting in the lobby of the Accra's Golden Tulip Hotel, Hiro Hattori, then chief of education at the Ghana office of UNICEF, explained the situation as it stood in 2009. "Ghana has done a good job in expanding access to primary schools," he said. "More children are attending school, but that has had an impact on the quality of the education they are receiving. Not only is the percentage of trained teachers declining, but class sizes are increasing and availability of school texts and materials isn't keeping up." Serious too is the decline in teacher attendance. "The average absentee rate among teachers is presently at 27 percent. This means that many hours are wasted because of teachers being absent, or coming late. So the students spend very little time in actual learning."

In a paper issued in 2008 entitled "Education Sector Performance," the government announced plans to address the situation. "They intend to start by strengthening the head teacher's skills in areas of management and supervision," Hiro Hattori continued. "Most of the head teachers have had no training in leadership or in management. They also plan to strengthen each school community so that local communities can and will take more action to help improve the performance of schools in their neighbourhood. And finally, they plan to increase the supply of teaching materials."

Added to the problem is the fact that the mayor of Accra, anxious to remove the 'shift system' whereby pupils attended school either in the morning or the afternoon, decided to enforce full-day school for all.

On the brighter side, following the lifting of school fees at the primary school level in 2005, the Ghanaian Education Service has called for the building of more schools, the improvement of existing schools, the training of more teachers and has pledged to provide textbooks on core subjects for all primary school pupils. At the time of writing, there were already signs that they are expanding existing schools in some corners of Accra. It remains to be seen when and if the other plans will be fulfilled.

THE MORE KATHY BECAME FAMILIAR WITH THE SITUATION IN THE schools, the more she began to feel she could make as big a contribution there as she was making with her libraries. She had already visited dozens of primary schools in Accra so she knew first-hand about the sad state of education at that level. She also recognized that the dismal standard of primary education was the main cause of low literacy rates in Ghana, not only among children but among teens and adults who had never had a chance to attend school or who had finished school with minimal skills. Girls were the most seriously affected since they were traditionally kept home to help with younger siblings or to carry out other household chores. That was the spark that started Kathy's far-reaching work with dozens of the primary schools in Accra.

The situation in many of Ghana's schools was then, and still is, far from ideal. Storybooks are scarce, at best, classrooms are crowded and teachers stressed. Kathy remembered her school visits with Faith Avis who was impressed by the effect of Kathy's presence. "She walks into these schools where the children have nothing, where some of them are writing with chalk on the cement floor and their faces light up the minute she steps into the classroom. She comes in with her incredible enthusiasm and the most important thing she brings is hope—hope that things can be improved, that these kids can have a better chance in life."

Ever since her first visit to Ringway School, Kathy tried to visit as many schools as she could, encouraging the teachers, bringing them books, reading to the students, trying her best to help nurture young readers. At each school, she would start in one classroom, stand in front of the students and read them a story, holding up the book so they could see the pictures. Then she would ask them questions. "Do you like this story?" A few shy nods. "Who is your favourite character in this book? Do you like the drawings? Would you like another story?" "Yes, yes," would come shouts from all around the classroom. Then she would show them how to turn the pages, carefully lifting the top corner. "I tell the teachers that it doesn't matter if the students don't understand the English words. Turning the pages and looking at the pictures is the beginning of the reading process." Wherever there was teacher support and interest, she would leave behind a few books, encourage them to follow her example and urge them to read to their pupils every day.

Kathy found the school project so fruitful that she tried to visit as many as she could. The point of these visits was two-fold: it offered encouragement to the teachers and demonstrated to them the importance of reading. It also showed the students that reading could be fun.

More and more schools came under Kathy's spell. One shining example is St. Kizito Primary School in Nima. Kathy had already stopped by the school in 1998 and found that the only books the students knew were the well-thumbed classroom textbooks which they had to share with as many as 80 other students. Not one of the students had ever seen a storybook. Before leaving, she had given each classroom a few books. Their response was so enthusiastic, she returned with more books and wooden cabinets to store them in.

A visit she made to the school two years later in May 2000 speaks volumes about the special relationship that developed between them. Kathy and I were leaving for the airport for our return to Canada and we decided to stop at the school to say goodbye. As our taxi wheeled into the school courtyard for our unannounced visit, a teacher spotted Kathy and alerted the others. In a flash, all the teachers rushed over to engulf her in hugs. Then each one in turn led her to their classroom where the students jumped to their feet and greeted her with loud rhythmic clapping.

In the first classroom, the pupils all stood up smartly at attention. "Good afternoon," said Kathy. "Good afternoon Madam Katty," they repeated in unison. "How many of you have read a book this week?" asked Kathy. Every single hand shot up. "Which are your favourite books," she asked. One student after another stood up and, very seriously, stated their favourite titles. "That's just great," said Kathy. Then she moved to the next classroom for more of the same.

When it was time to leave, Kathy climbed into her waiting taxi and, as it pulled away, the teachers and students hung from every door and window waving. Not long after that visit, Kathy received a letter from a Grade 6 teacher. "The library books you brought us, the children love them so much that, when they take one, they want to finish it before it is time for assembly. If they cannot finish it, they hold it under their desks and continue reading while the teacher is speaking."

Kathy later reflected on her visit to St. Kizito and smiled at the memory. "I can't tell you how proud I was to see all those children reading," she said. "When I first visited them two years ago, those children had never seen a storybook. Just look at the transformation!"

The results of these school visits, especially those she made to the most deprived state schools, were easily apparent. Mercia Laryea, the former assistant director of education for the Ghana Education Service, heaps praises on Kathy's initiative. "Thanks to her, there is now ample evidence that the development of reading in schools has begun to take off. It is such a joy to see these children acquiring the habit of reading and, more important, enjoying what they read."

Emma Amoo-Gottfried, one of the OCLF's two Ghanaian directors and headmistress of Faith Montessori, a large private school in Ghana, agrees. "Her presence in those schools is an enormous encouragement to teachers who receive meagre pay, who never have any reading materials, and who are often completely discouraged," she said. "With her infectious enthusiasm, she has brought so much excitement into so many classrooms. In fact, she is the greatest possible gift to the Ghana Education Service."

Encouraged by the positive results of bringing books into the schools, Kathy decided to use her libraries as springboards for literacy training for older students, teens and adults who had never had the chance to learn to read and write. In 1994, she decided to set up free literacy classes in the library in Osu and tacked up a sign on the gate welcoming all to the library on Tuesday and Thursday mornings. Classes would be taught in English, Ghana's official language. Given that there are more than 75 different languages spoken around the country, most people see the knowledge of English as their best hope for employment.

It was a stroke of good luck that a woman from England who was living in Accra at the time offered to help launch those first classes. Gina Holly was a trained TEFL (Teaching English as a Foreign Language) instructor so she was the perfect person to welcome the newcomers and help set up the appropriate groups. Kathy also hired Florence Acheampong, a Ghanaian woman, to work hand-in-hand with Gina. She was aware that Gina wasn't in Ghana for long and it was vital that the Ghanaians learned her teaching methods. By the time Gina left, Florence had picked up most of the basics.

Days after Kathy had posted the sign on the gate, 14 students turned up for the first class, mostly older women, some of whom were parents of library members. Then a few teenagers began to trickle in. These were girls who had been sent down to Accra as young children from their villages in the North to work as household help for a relative. They spent their days minding the children, cleaning the house, going to market and preparing meals. Their employers saw them as indispensable and, since they were usually girls, school was out of the question. As they became teenagers, they started to realize what they had missed.

The stories of these students were often heartbreaking. At first, they found it difficult even to enter the library and face a room full of strangers. They were intensely shy and ashamed that they could not read or write. They had all come from problem situations; the fact that they'd never had the chance to go to school spoke volumes. But at the library, they soon discovered that these classes were not only places to learn reading and writing, they were also places of fellowship. Here, they were welcomed warmly by the staff. Here, they could share their stories with others and realize that they were not alone. Says Kathy: "I felt so badly for these young people. Many of them had real talent but they never had the chance to develop it."

The literacy classes at the Osu Library have continued to be enormously popular. At the time of writing, they are held two mornings a week from 10 a.m. to 12 p.m. and are attracting more than 35 students each week. The students range in age from 16 upwards. James, a 72-year-old fisherman, has been attending for more than two years, turns up early and stays late and has rarely missed a class. Many of them travel more than an hour from the far end of the city and often arrive an hour early to help sweep the compound or to delve into their notebooks.

Joanna divides them according to their level—beginners, intermediate and advanced. Library staff members teach the classes, while volunteers, many drawn from the expatriate community, help out. When each student completes one level, they receive a certificate and move on to the next. "It is sort of like a club without officially calling itself a club," Kathy points out. "The camaraderie that develops among the students is so special."

At one of the classes recently, Kathy watched Rachel, a woman in her twenties, struggling to write her name. After carefully trying to pen each letter, she finally managed to write all the letters of her name—for the first time. Said Kathy: "It is so empowering for a person to be able to write their name. Otherwise, her identity is only a thumb print."

Legions of success stories have sprung from these classes. Some students who have gained new literacy skills have finally been able to enter or return to school. Others have managed to set up small businesses. Many delight in being able to write a full sentence, to fill out a cheque, or read stories to their children.

Seven years after the first literacy classes began at the Osu Library, Khadijah Forkor, an attractive young woman, was 18 when she first walked through the library gate. She was clearly bright, but unable to read or write even her own name. Khadijah's story is similar to that of many learners: she felt shy and ashamed when she stepped through the gate but she gradually began to feel at ease with the others and soon she felt free to talk about herself.

She had grown up in a small village and, as a child, had been obliged to help her mother sell charcoal in the local market. She was barely five when she was sent to live with her aunt in Accra. Her aunt expected her to do all the household chores, to fetch the water, clean the house, shop and cook all the meals and even look after her children. School was not an option.

Every morning, Khadijah would bathe the children and take them to school. "There, I saw all the children playing together and I cried inside my heart because I wanted to join them. I so wanted to go to school but I wasn't allowed." By the time she reached her teens, she was able to earn a little money selling vegetables. But it wasn't enough. She grew increasingly restless.

Khadijah recalls the day when she first heard about the literacy classes. She beams at the memory. "I was so happy to go to the library and to learn to read and write. I didn't want to be selling any more. I wanted to be someone. I wanted to be like the women I saw on television."

She turned up at her classes regularly twice a week. She worked hard, first learning the alphabet, then sounding out two and three-letter words. The real breakthrough came when she learned to write her name. "Khadijah is a hard name to spell," she said, as she picked up a pencil and carefully wrote the letters of her name. "At first, I had to concentrate very hard and spell out each letter. But when I was finally able to write my name, it made me very happy because saying my name without knowing how to write it is very bad. It is not everybody who can spell 'Khadijah.' I am very proud."

The rewards for Khadijah were great. She could now write a shopping list before she went the market. She could also read the signboards. "When you know how to read and write, you know how to talk, to walk, to do everything in life."

It was the discovery of books that was the turning point for Khadijah. "I loved being able to read," she said. "When you are reading a story, it is as if you are talking to people." As she speaks, she leafs through a book of fairy tales called *Sleepy Time Stories*. "The two stories I love best are *Cinderella* and *Snow White*. I love them because the way these stories go is like what I have gone through in my life. I love especially the story of Snow White, how she is treated by her stepmother. Cinderella too. In the end, they all won." Khadijah pauses on the final page and points to a picture of Cinderella riding off in a golden chariot with her handsome prince. "Maybe one day, I too will move forward," she says. Adds Kathy: "So many of our young literacy students identify with Cinderella. They want to meet and marry a prince and do better in the future."

For now, Khadijah is happy to sit curled up in a corner with an armful of books. "These stories make me realize that I am not alone," she says. "Someone else is like me. I read to forget my problems. And when I read, I am happy and laughing, as if I am talking to somebody."

Khadijah once confided in me that more than anything in the world, she would like to become a lawyer. "That way, I feel I could help people," she said. "But that's a long way off." Soon after our conversation, her mother, who had been ill for some time, died of AIDS. Khadijah was devastated. "Now I am completely alone," she sighed. "When I wake up, there is nobody there to say 'How are you ?' I wish to have a mother because it is the mother who will say 'My child, how are you feeling?' And that is what I have not had in my life since I was a child. But now the teachers at the library are my mothers. And so is Auntie Kathy."

Khadijah learned well enough to enter a government junior high school (JHS) and was not intimidated to be years older than her classmates. She managed to complete JHS successfully. In 2010, she gave birth to Joseph, a baby boy, and in 2012, a baby girl called Michelle, named after Michelle Smulders, a Canadian expatriate volunteer who gave her special help. She hopes someday to return to school to finish her education. She still struggles on many fronts but clearly she is a happier, more confident woman, now calling herself 'Princess.'

"When I first met Kathy, she welcomed me into her heart," says Khadijah, tears welling up in her eyes. "She helped me to read and to get back into school. With her advice and her encouragement, she made me understand that my education was so important. For that I love her so much."

THE LITERACY CLASSES AT THE KATHY KNOWLES COMMUNITY LIBRARY were so successful that Kathy started offering similar classes at the Nima Library. She wasn't sure how to begin so she visited her friend Agnes Amoah, the same women who had given her the land for the Nima Library. Agnes gathered together a group of women from Nima who met in her courtyard. Kathy asked them if they wanted to learn to read and write. They all nodded. Most of them came from the North so she asked them if they wanted lessons in *Hausa*, their first language, in *Twi*, the most widely-spoken language in Ghana, or in English. They all opted for English, the official language of business and government.

The next day, a delegation of women— primarily drain cleaners and market traders—turned up at the library eager to start. They were mostly Muslim women of all ages who, if they could write at all, did so using the Arabic script and moved from right to left on the page. The literacy classes soon attracted both men and woman and teenagers. Under the watchful eye of librarian Kate Akwa, the beginners would spend hours trying to master a single letter, each time proudly showing it to Kate for approval. When one 65-year-old woman first arrived, she didn't even know how to hold a pencil but slowly, very slowly, she learned to spell her name. With their newly acquired skills, a few of these hard-working students have managed to find jobs.

In early 2012, when some of the younger women were dropping out of class to care for their babies, Hannah Agyeman, the librarian-in-charge, invited them to bring their babies and pre-school children with them to class and she set up a mini-daycare at one end of the room. So five tiny children played happily with blocks and stuffed animals while their mothers were honing their writing skills. Hannah loves acting as the perfect grandmother and has even supplied a few small board books to start them on the road to reading.

The stories of these late-learners illustrate the profound effect of the literacy classes. Hanatu, a seamstress, recognized that if she wished to start a business, she needed to learn to read and write. She attended classes regularly and within months, she was able to record measurements, write a shopping list, and prepare an invoice.

Barikusu, a Muslim woman of about 55, was one of the first to join the class. For years, she came faithfully every Tuesday and Thursday morning, sat at the same table and very gradually improved.

One day, she arrived at class with some big news. She had just returned from a pilgrimage to Mecca, and while waiting for her luggage to arrive on the conveyor belt, a man had reached out and grabbed her container of holy water. "That holy water is mine," she shouted. The man held on tight and said "No," it was his. Barikusu then proceeded to spell her name which was written on the side of the container. Surprised, the man returned it but asked how she knew it was hers. Barikusu told him she had learned to read at the Nima Library.

As the classes progressed, they attracted more and more people from all walks of life including recently-arrived immigrants from across West Africa and from war-torn Sudan. Slowly, their skills developed and they learned to sign their names, to read a contract, or write a cheque. For those who are parents, this new skill has helped them to nurture their own children's education. One young mother spoke of her delight at being able to read to her children for the first time in her life.

After very few months, these women have acquired skills that enhance their self-esteem and serve them well. Kate Akwa, the librarian in charge of the Nima Library literacy classes, is an encouraging presence for the new learners and praises each step forward. "None of us could have guessed that learning to read and write could give these women such confidence, improve their job prospects and, most importantly, help to empower them as women."

Approximately 2,500 illiterate teens and adults have already benefited from the OCLF literacy classes since they began in 1994. Based on the success of the libraries' daytime classes, the Nima Maamobi Community Learning Centre, another of Kathy's initiatives that opened in 2006 tucked behind the Nima Library, formed evening literacy groups. These run four nights a week and are led by enthusiastic Ghanaian teachers including former library members. An average of 35 working people turn up each evening, many of them crossing the city for the chance to learn how to read.

"This literacy program is one of Kathy's most far-reaching projects," says Emma Amoo-Gottfried who has personally witnessed many of the classes. "It is magical when you see the transformation of these people who are shy and ashamed when they arrive. They become happy and confident and their faces light up when they say 'Now I can read.'

"Kathy has brought laughter to the faces of thousands of women. She has empowered them. Suddenly, with new knowledge and new skills, they can take control of their lives. Not only is she educating a woman, but that woman now wants to make sure that her children are educated too. And what is even more important is that, as in all her ventures, Kathy is setting an example. She is showing what can be done with relatively few resources. People from all over the country are learning from her."

## CHAPTER 9

# More Libraries Take Root

IF ANYONE THINKS ABOUT GHANA AT ALL, IT IS USUALLY AS THE BIRTH-place and home of Kofi Annan, secretary general of the United Nations from 1997 to 2006 and the winner, with the UN, of the 2001 Nobel Peace Prize.

Others might be more familiar with the fact that Ghana boasts a surprisingly strong football (soccer) team, *The Black Stars,* which brought the country—and the whole continent—world-wide recognition when they reached the quarter finals in the 2010 World Cup football tournament in South Africa. Notable too was their junior team, the *Under 20's,* who won acclaim when they snatched up the World Cup in 2009.

Those with longer memories might recall that the most significant date in Ghana's history was on March 6, 1957 when the country, then known as the Gold Coast, became the first country in sub-Saharan Africa to gain its independence from Britain. At the handing-over ceremony, the Duchess of Kent, who represented Queen Elizabeth, told the gathering that "the hopes of many, especially in Africa, hang on your endeavours…" At the stroke of midnight, Britain's Union Jack was lowered and the new flag of Ghana—three stripes of red, gold and green plus a black star—was hoisted in its place. The crowds sang and danced in Parliament Square as Kwame Nkrumah, their new young leader, stepped onto the podium. Under the glare of floodlights, he declared to all that "Ghana, your beloved country, is free forever." Euphoria gripped the whole country.

No other African state has been launched into independence with such promise. Nkrumah, just 47, was a charismatic figure and was considered a leader of outstanding ability. He was a true visionary and a strong proponent for African unity, together with Julius Nyerere, president of what, in 1964, became Tanzania. He gave generous financial support to other newly-independent countries and was the prime mover behind the formation of the Organization of African Unity (OAU) in 1963. An early statue of Nkrumah in Accra recognized his Pan-African dream by carrying the message "The independence of Ghana is meaningless without the independence of all Africa."

Under his watch, Nkrumah was responsible for building the Akosombo Hydroelectric Dam and a large aluminum smelting industry. He built roads and a deepwater harbour at Tema. He expanded the education system which was then ranked among the best in Africa, thanks largely to the legacy of the British.

When Nkrumah took office, Ghana was one of the richest tropical countries in the world, with vast resources of cocoa, gold, timber and bauxite that were all in great demand. The future looked promising for the country and their president provided a beacon of hope, not only for his own countrymen but for black people all over Africa.

In less than a decade, however, those hopes began to fade. By early 1966, Nkrumah had banned all opposition parties, declaring himself 'President for Life.' He also began arresting and imprisoning his political opponents. He then tried to extend his control over the military and that became the final blow. Few were surprised, in February 1966, when he was on a state visit to North Vietnam and China, that he was deposed by a military coup.

Nkrumah never returned to Ghana but lived in exile in Guinea. In failing health, he flew to Romania for medical treatment and died there of skin cancer in 1972 at the age of 62. His remains were returned to Accra and were buried, along with those of his wife, in a modest tomb in Nkroful, the village of his birth. They were later transferred to the Kwame Nkrumah Mausoleum that dominates a large memorial park in downtown Accra.

There followed a long period of disarray with one military dictator overthrowing another, each one more corrupt than the last. During the 1970s, they expelled all foreign workers, impoverished their own farmers and plotted coup after coup. Added to all this were two serious droughts and a soaring inflation rate. It was a demoralizing period for Ghanaians and it prompted a huge exodus of professionals—doctors and surgeons, teachers and nurses—a brain drain that is still felt today.

Some hope was restored with the arrival of Flight Lieutenant Jerry John (called J.J. or 'Junior Jesus' by some). Rawlings, a little-known half-Ghanaian, half-Scottish air force officer, who seized power in 1979. The first ten years of his rule were depressing as well while he ruled with an iron fist. OLCF board member Florence Adjepong looks back on the mid-1980s, when she first arrived in Ghana from England with her Ghanaian husband, as one of the worst periods of political upheaval. She remembers shortages of everything, especially food, forcing them to lead a hand-to-mouth existence. There were also constant light and water outages. "We spent most evenings in the dark with no lights, no water," she sighs at the thought. "It was just like camping, though without food supplies. The only thing that helped us was our faith. Without that, we would never have survived."

Rawlings eventually learned to be a populist leader rather than a dictator. In 1992, under the banner of his National Democratic Congress (NDC) party, he surprised many by removing his military uniform and running for president as a civilian in the first democratically held election in years. He served as president for two terms and willingly stepped down when they were up in 2000.

The election that followed saw John Kufour of the New Patriotic Party (NPP) defeat Jerry Rawlings' hand-picked candidate, John Atta Mills. Eight years later, in a closely-fought but peaceful election in December 2008, the tables were turned and the formerly unsuccessful Mr. Mills eked out a narrow victory over the incumbent John Kufour to become Ghana's third president.

KATHY ARRIVED BACK IN GHANA IN FEBRUARY 2000, ANXIOUS TO CHECK on the progress of the Nima Library opened two years before. It was the same year that John Kufour and the NPP had come to power and hopes were riding high. The morning after she arrived, she stopped at the Nima Library and found that it was still running well with dozens of children entering its doors each day. Already, there was a special atmosphere in the place that no one could have predicted. The children were well-behaved, they were respectful of the building and, perhaps most important, they were respectful of the books. She was especially happy to notice that the place was spotlessly clean, a sizeable task when the annual Harmattan sand storms had recently swept through the country coating everything in dust.

Kathy also spent time with Joanna in her library and visited no fewer than 36 schools and several new library projects both in Accra and beyond. One was in Tamale, capital of the Northern Region and a 10 hour (650 km) drive north of Accra. Frank Cosway, a semi-retired Canadian businessman who was then living in Tamale, encouraged her to apply for a $45,000 grant from the Canadian International Development Agency (CIDA) to help renovate a badly-neglected and time-worn children's library in the centre of town and equip some 25 smaller rural community libraries in outlying villages. Now that she had two successful libraries to her credit, CIDA was willing to grant her request.

Frank Cosway agreed to co-ordinate the project and worked on it for four years. He supervised the renovation of the downtown children's library and then addressed the needs of the surrounding countryside. "We spent much of our time helping the different communities to plan and manage a children's library," he said. "This involved organizing monthly meetings, visiting the sites regularly, preparing detailed reports on the projects for CIDA. I learned a lot from Kathy's example about how to run an exciting children's community library."

AS KATHY TOURED THE COUNTRY TO ENCOURAGE SMALL INITIATIVES and launch new ones, she became even more aware of the thousands of children who had never seen or held a storybook. One evening as she sat in her bedroom, she took out a notebook and calculated that her modest fundraising campaigns were now bringing in a steady income. With a little more effort and a certain amount of luck, she might be able to raise enough funds to build another library. The more she thought about it, the more she thought "Why stop here?"

Quite by chance, she received a call the next day from the member of Parliament for Mamprobi, a community in downtown Accra. He had visited the Nima Library, was very impressed by it and was calling to see if Kathy would build a library in his own community. A piece of land was available next to a school and the municipality was willing to donate it to the project. Furthermore, they were also prepared to supply the all-important letter agreeing to pay all the staff salaries and utility bills.

Kathy jumped in a taxi at once and when she saw the land, she knew it would work well for a library. Mamprobi was a poor fishing community with several large schools and no library. She met with local officials the next day to discuss the project and they were excited at the prospect of having a library of their own.

Kathy returned to Canada bent on raising the estimated $62,000 she needed for the new project. She was about to start another fundraising campaign when she learned that an article about her work in Ghana would be appearing in the March 2001 Canadian edition of *Reader's Digest*. "The timing was perfect," she recalled. "I couldn't have asked for anything better."

The minute the magazine hit the newsstands, with Kathy's smiling face peering out from the cover, over 200 letters poured into her mailbox. They included cheques and books, notes of congratulation and words of encouragement. Entire communities across Canada and beyond mustered up forces to raise funds. Two Winnipeg choirs planned fundraising events. A Girl Guide company in Guelph, Ontario, launched a book-collecting campaign. A church in Walkerton, another Ontario town, donated the proceeds of their 'Hunger Meal,' a fundraising event whereby visitors dine on a small bowl of soup to remind them of others who are less fortunate. And a 76-year-old woman delivered a cheque to Kathy's house in Winnipeg after she spotted the article in her doctor's office. She discretely 'borrowed' the magazine, she explained, copied out the address and returned it to her doctor.

The post brought more surprises every week. A stamp collector from Chilliwack, B.C. sent two pounds of stamps for the Nima Library's stamp club. A Ghanaian woman living in Waterloo, Ontario, tucked a cheque inside a note which read: "Your story transported me back to when I was a young child in Ghana. I have had lots of helping hands along the way. It is now time to 'pass it on' in the hopes that others can be helped as I have been."

The article also prompted letters from around the world, many of them seeking help or advice on how to build a library in their own community or village. One carefully-penned note arrived from Sister Natividad, a Catholic nun who lived in a remote corner of the Philippines, three hours by plane from the capital. She wrote "Would you consider sharing the joy of reading with our children in the Philippines?" She had long dreamed of opening a library for street children but was unsure about how to begin. Kathy replied immediately, sending off the relevant information and shipping a fifty pound carton of books. Into the pages of one of the books, she tucked a US $100 bill.

The minute the package reached the Philippines, Sister Nativadad sent a glowing note back. "A journey of a thousand miles starts with the first step and you were there to help us make the first step," she wrote. "Congratulations on the great work you have done to push back the frontiers of ignorance among poor children of our world. We shall try to move heaven and earth to have these children 'get wild about reading'." She named her tiny library "The Children's Library of Hope." It continues to this day.

KATHY WAS NOW TRAVELLING TO GHANA TWICE A YEAR SO SHE ARRIVED back in Ghana that November armed with a greatly improved bank balance and set to work on the new Mamprobi Library. She had learned much from her experience with the earlier libraries. She now knew much better what is involved in every stage of the construction process, the importance of finding a reliable contractor and trustworthy workmen, the time-consuming details required to finish the job so she now felt she had the confidence to start again. She asked Michel van den Nieuwenhof, a Dutch architect then living in Ghana, to design the building. She knew his ideas matched hers—natural surfaces, rounded edges, lots of curves. Following Kathy's wishes, he chose to cover the cement building blocks with laterite, a light brown adobe-like surface which, Kathy points out, is very practical since it doesn't ever need painting.

She then met Kojo Maclean, a genial Ghanaian, who became the project supervisor. She was also buoyed by the loyalty of two of her workmen: Bright, the soft-spoken and gifted mason who had worked on the Nima Library, and, for the paint job, Theophilus Tsede, who would become her most trusted painter for all the interior walls and ceilings, doors and window frames. Both agreed to help with the new project. "These two are the most dedicated people I know," said Kathy. "They both know that I expect perfection and they work hard to achieve it, thus taking their trades to a higher level." In fact, Kathy felt honoured to be invited to the 'outdooring' ceremony of Bright's baby daughter, Matilda . The 'outdooring' is a traditional rite of passage, an occasion to name the new baby eight days after her birth and a chance for family and friends to welcome the new child into their midst.

Bright and Theophilus had already learned much by working on Kathy's earlier projects. Bright knew that winding pathways are more interesting than straight ones: they add an element of invitation to the building. He also saw that by inserting broken tiles into a pathway or a bench, you can create interesting designs. At another library Bright helped to build, he quite independently wrote the words 'Share a Non-Stop Book Journey' using broken coloured tiles fixed into the main pathway that wound up to the front door. The fact that he has had little formal education didn't deter him from using his considerable artistic skills.

With proceeds that came after the release of the *Reader's Digest* article and the generosity of more Canadians including, once again, the Gale family, Kathy had the necessary funds to complete, furnish and supply books for the Mamprobi Library. On June 20, 2001, less than a year after the sod was turned, Kathy and the local chief cut the ribbon to officially open the Mamprobi Gale Community Library. Guardian of the property is a Ghanaian-carved wooden statue of Pooh Bear, hero of the popular children's book *Winnie the Pooh*, and a World's Ambassador of Friendship as declared by Nane Annan, wife of former UN Secretary General Kofi Annan. Termites later devoured much of Pooh's midsection, but he has now been replaced by a new and more robust version and wears the same benevolent smile to welcome library visitors.

THE COASTAL ROAD EAST FROM ACCRA TO NUNGUA IS KNOWN FOR THREE things: spectacular seaside vistas with ocean waves pounding against the shore, congested traffic at any time of day, and Ghana's most inventive builders of coffins who live and work in the seaside village of Teshie.

These specially-commissioned coffins are designed to have some connection to the life of the departed and their popularity has grown over the years. The makers count among their commissions a coffin shaped like a fish carved for a deceased fisherman, a plane for a former pilot, a syringe for a nurse and a beer bottle for a renowned drinker.

From the road, you can spot a taxi-shaped coffin built for a one-time taxi driver, a mobile phone for a businessman, a hammer for a carpenter and, best of all, a Mercedes for a businessman, sporting a licence plate with the letters R.I.P. (Rest in Peace).

The town of Nungua, home of OCLF's next and most beautiful library, lies just beyond the coffin world, about five kilometres east of Accra. The sprawling Nungua Community Library was built in 2003 for just under $150,000 and Kathy commissioned Michel van den Nieuwenhof, the same architect who worked on the Mamprobi Library, to design the building. This library, more than any other, reflects Kathy's personal touch: the circular shape and the warm earth-tones of the exterior, the vaulted ceiling and the bright blue wooden trim adorning every window, roof line and doorway. There is the signature winding pathway that leads to the front door, an ivory gardenia bush Kathy planted in memory of her grandmother, a mahogany tree, a cinnamon tree and more than 250 bougainvillea seedlings circling the compound. Kathy's attention to detail is everywhere: in the staff washroom, the wall is decorated with small ceramic tiles donated by her friend Helen List, each one showing a picture of a pig, a lamb or a rooster.

The library stands within sight of several large schools and serves a population of about 10,000 students. After school, at break time, at weekends and especially on school holidays, the children—as many as 250 at a time— flock to the building, remove their shoes and pass under an archway that reads "Imagination is more important than knowledge (Albert Einstein)." The younger children choose a book and sit at round tables on the lower level and the older ones move to the upper level where they have access to shelves of school texts and reference books.

The minute the library opened, it became an important fixture in the community. Kathy named Abigail Elisha as head librarian, the same woman who brought her two small children to Kathy's first reading circle. Abigail has a quiet, soft-spoken manner, rarely raises her voice and runs her library with clock-like precision. Kathy seizes any chance to sing her praises. "Abigail had worked with Joanna for two years so she had good experience, had learned much about libraries and what makes them work. She is quite simply another jewel."

Afternoon story times at the Nungua Library are always popular and outside a large frangipani tree (called "forget-me-not" in Ghana), its branches laden with creamy white blossoms, provides shade for an open theatre space where older students practice and perform cultural dancing and drumming.

In November 2007, the Nungua Library received a surprise visit from reporter David Gutnik of the Canadian Broadcasting Corporation He dropped by to record a radio report for the CBC's *Sounds Like Canada* program. Speaking to host Shelagh Rogers and to hundreds of listeners across Canada, David bubbled with enthusiasm about the place. "When I reached Accra, someone told me that there was another Canadian—an *'Obruni'* they call white people—who was doing these wonderful things in some of the poorest corners of the city. When I heard that she was visiting the Nungua Library that day, I climbed in a cab, wound along the seaside and ended up here. When I walked into that library, my jaw just dropped. What a beautiful place it is with its soaring cathedral ceiling, rows of big windows and tiled floors.

"I was welcomed by 10-year-old Precious, a library member since she was six. 'You must leave your shoes here,' she told me. 'We don't want to dirty the floor'." David missed the cue and neglected to remove his shoes. Precious didn't comment. "Also," Precious continued in a whisper, "if you come into the library, you must be very quiet."

Before he had a chance to move inside, Kathy appeared and David steered her over to stand under the frangipani tree. "Whatever keeps you doing this, year after year?" he asked her. "What is your motivation?"

"Well," she replied, "children love to read and it is through their enthusiasm that I am trying to meet their needs. That is all." "And what challenges do you face?" asked David. "I spend my life dealing with challenges," she replied. "There are always things such as leaking roofs, broken tiles, quirky plumbing. There are always staff issues to deal with. But we are lucky to have excellent staff. The strength of our libraries really rests with the people who run them."

There is a pause while David adjusts his microphone. Kathy continues. "The most important thing is to build confidence in the community. We have many meetings with the elders, the assemblymen or women, the local MP's. I never work independently. All that has to be in sync or nothing happens. Yes, the challenges can be great, but you just keep plodding along and eventually things work out."

While she is speaking, the children gather to welcome the visitors with a succession of poems and songs. David clearly loved it all as he sat cross-legged on the floor among the children. "At the end of the performance, Kathy couldn't just sit and watch," he told his radio audience. "She jumped to her feet and sang and danced with the rest of them. It was a magical moment."

David also got up and danced with the children. "What a day that was," he enthused. "I saw at once what a difference the library is making in that community." At the end of his report, David received a sound "tsk tsk" from CBC host, Shelagh Rogers. "Next time, David, you must not forget to remove your shoes!"

EACH OF KATHY'S LIBRARIES HAS ITS OWN CHARACTER AND THE ONE she chose to build in the tiny fishing village of Goi, 70 kilometres east of Accra on a turnoff from the main highway to neighbouring Togo, is no exception. As is the case with all the seaside communities which rely on fishing for their livelihood, times are tough as large foreign vessels continue to ease out the local and much smaller fleets.

The decision to build a library in this small village was due, in large part, to the energy and enthusiasm of Vivian Amanor, a dynamic woman who was determined to help the children of her village, especially those who were unable to attend school. In 2000, a former citizen of Goi had seen the KKCL Library in Osu and wanted the same for his village. Vivian was the perfect choice to be the librarian and she travelled to Accra for training with Joanna. She returned home with a box of books to boost her tiny collection.

One day, Vivian invited a few of the children to the veranda of her home where she read them stories from her small collection of books. They loved it but before long, the group became too large for her veranda. She made inquiries and finally received permission to use an abandoned fish-smoking hut on the beach, shaded from the sun and wind by a grove of tall palm trees. At first, she loaded her few books into a wooden wagon and dragged what she called her "library on wheels" down to the shelter.

She worked long hours with little support from the community and no pay. "At times, I felt like giving up," Vivian admitted. "But then I thought about the children and I knew that this was the best thing I could give them. The small education I received as a child, I was now able to use to educate my community."

Each passing week, more and more children appeared at Vivian's beach-front library. Once again, she was soon running out of space so pressed the authorities to allow her to use an empty classroom in the local government school. She had just received the go-ahead when Noreen Mian, a Canadian from Winnipeg who was looking for 'a slower, more creative pace of life,' arrived in Goi to help as a volunteer with the project. She had barely unpacked her bags when she jumped into action helping Vivian and a friend transform the dusty classroom into a library. They painted the walls, covered the ceiling with grass mats and hung up dream-catcher mobiles laced with feathers and sea shells. Kathy was so happy with the results that, on her next visit, she handed over several more boxes of books and provided funds for tables and chairs and shelves. Before long, more than 100 children were squeezing into the tiny room to enjoy stories and books.

"It was pandemonium at first," recalls Noreen. "The children were so excited they wanted to do everything all at once. So we devised a schedule and designated two days for games and the other days for books and puzzles." Then Noreen created a Reading Tree, a cardboard image of a tree, tacked it to the wall. She then urged every student to read a book then write the name of the book on a mango leaf and pin it to the tree. "It was a great way to get the kids reading."

Local officials soon came to realize they had a precious resource in their midst and agreed to provide a small salary for Vivian. With this support from the community, together with Vivian's proven commitment, Kathy decided to build a freestanding library for the village. The new library is a handsome adobe-style structure nestled among a grove of coconut palm trees. The community chose to name the building the Kathy Knowles Community Library, Goi , and it opened in June 2008 with a lively celebration of music and dancing.

Word spread quickly and teachers from all over the region began to transport their classes to the library to enjoy the books, organize Scrabble competitions and support the enthusiastic theatre group. Almost overnight, the new library clearly put Goi on the map. Most important of all is the fact that, less than a year after the library opened, the school grades of the students who had been using it regularly soared upwards. Kathy beamed when she heard the news. "Those are the sort of rewards that keep me going."

Vivian herself is an avid reader and is therefore an important role model for the children in her village. She reads every book that comes into the library and begs for more—"specially those inspirational ones." She has had a difficult past, bringing up four children as a single mother, and says that books help her forget those difficult days. "A storybook takes you into a different world, helps you become what you want to be," she once told me. "We are suffering too much. We need those books to help us."

Whenever Kathy visits Goi, she asks the older children to write letters of thanks to her Canadian donors. This has become an important ritual at all her libraries. One child in Goi wrote recently that "Our library is a magic place. Through our books, we can walk the African plains and see elephants and zebras, giraffes and feel the hot sun. Here, you can go anywhere in the whole wide world." Another child wrote: "I am happy to express my profane (*sic*) gratitude for your sincere love, empathy, tolerance you have shown us. Tears wipe from my face by bringing us this library." And finally, from a 14-year-old : "Goi is a nice town near the ocean. The sea roars at night when everyone is asleep. Sometimes it even plays music."

## CHAPTER 10

# *Birth of the Nima Maamobi Community Learning Centre*

ALL THE LIBRARIES KATHY HAD BUILT IN GHANA WERE FUNCTIONING well. But her brain was already churning over another idea, this one with a different twist.

The idea she was hatching came about in a curious way. The moment of revelation occurred in October 2002 when Britain's Queen Elizabeth visited Winnipeg as part of her Golden Jubilee tour of Canada and Kathy attended a celebration in her honour at the Legislative Building. The ceremony included a loud fanfare, lively music and dancing. That was the spark and she woke the next morning with an exciting idea. She joined a neighbour for an early morning run and shared her dream of creating a place in Nima where library members could also showcase their many talents—their dancing, drumming, and theatre skills. "The more I talked about it, the more I thought to myself 'Wow. Wouldn't that be neat!' " Then, another thought sprang to mind. A reading hall upstairs would be a fitting add-on to the facility to meet the needs of the senior youth who had graduated from the smaller Nima Library and who had limited space to study in their crowded and badly-lit homes.

That same morning, Kathy phoned Ghana and spoke to K.D. Osei, the metro director of Town and Country Planning to share her idea and seek his support. Two weeks later, she received a faxed message from him including his endorsement of her plan. She also ran it past Hannah and she too was enthusiastic. Months later, when all the necessary permits were in place, Kathy began thinking up fundraising ideas to raise the estimated $400,000 she needed to realize this ambitious project. If building a library in Nima was a risk, this was an even bigger one. But Kathy was not shy of taking risks.

Once again, she needed to raise the funds. Encouraged to apply for another grant from the CIDA—the Canadian International Development Agency which helps finance many of Canada's foreign aid projects—she prepared a long and complicated proposal to cover part of the budget. But the request was turned down as being "too small" to consider. Kathy did later receive funding from CIDA for five short-term interns to work with her project but, by then, she had concluded that CIDA's requirements, which involved lengthy proposals and detailed progress reports, were far too demanding for a small NGO.

She then put her mind to more manageable fundraising ideas. She launched a "Chairs for Children Campaign." For $50, donors could honour a friend by having their name inscribed on a small brass plate to be tacked onto a chair or stool in the new centre. More than 450 chairs were named and they remain a fitting reminder of many donors and their friends. Next, she set up a "Buy a Block" campaign in Ghana to encourage members of the Nima community to donate towards the cost of a single block. She received 56 responses which was encouraging in such a poor community. She also devised a "Library-in-a-Bag" campaign, primarily for donors outside Ghana. With a $50 donation, a donor 'buys' a cloth Joy of Reading bag containing eight local storybooks, a cake of soap and a hand towel. These are given out to library members who help their librarians. For many children, especially those living in villages, the "Library-in-a-Bag" has given them their first chance to enjoy a book in their home. OCLF has already handed out more than 1,000 bags to delighted children.

Word spread about Kathy's ambitious new project and donations began to arrive, a few from Ghana but most from Canadians. She then contacted Roger Amenyogbe, a Ghanaian-born Canadian architect who then lived in Winnipeg. They talked for hours, exchanging ideas about the concept of the new building. Roger came up with an innovative design—a circular 6,000 square-foot two-storey building that, from one angle, looks like an open book. Inside, Roger explained, the trusses that support the roof are like the spreading branches of a tree. "In our tradition, that is where stories are told."

The two worked closely together for months, connecting almost weekly by phone or at a restaurant to fine tune all the details of the new facility. "Working with Kathy is an amazing experience," says Roger. "She approaches each project with such passion and dedication." He noted that, whenever she travels, Kathy is always on the lookout for different materials to incorporate into her newest library. In the case of the Nima Centre, it was a long, winding 140-foot-long bench that snakes across the courtyard. It was inspired by the work of the Spanish architect, Antoni Gaudi, whose buildings Kathy saw on a visit to Barcelona. Today, it is referred to as the 'Gaudi bench.'

Kathy then recruited her same loyal workmen to help with the project and hired Kojo Maclean to act again as project manager for the new building. "It is always quite an experience working with Kathy," smiled Kojo, a Ghanaian whose parents chose the name Maclean after an early British governor. "She sets very high standards and is on top of every single detail of every project—even when she is far away in Canada. Indeed, her attention to detail and her striving for perfection are a model for us all. Also," he adds, "it is such a treat to work with someone who always turns up on time! We have all learned a lot from her." Kathy too has learned from them and today, construction terms such as sloping soffits, joists and cornices. roof gutters and bills of quantities all roll off her tongue with ease.

The building rose slowly over the months ahead. As before, the workmen covered the cement blocks of the circular structure with the same laterite material. Her painter Theophilus didn't need to ask before painting every window frame, roofline and doorway bright blue. And along the borders of the fenced yard, the pink and orange bougainvillaea blossoms were already bursting into bloom as if to welcome the new building.

IN 2006, I SPENT THREE MONTHS IN ACCRA TO HELP MOVE THINGS along and ensure the building would be ready to open in November. As it began to take shape, there were dozens of details to attend to: floor tiles to buy, cushion covers to order, door knobs and locks to find, landscaping to organize. Almost daily, I travelled by taxi to the outskirts of Accra to pick up more supplies, more cement, more paint. There were continuous calls on our newly-acquired cell phone with a seemingly endless string of questions from the workmen, the electricians, the plumbers or the librarians.

There were also the usual hurdles that cropped up daily. A taxi would break down, supplies would run out, the tiler would constantly miscalculate his needs which meant another trip to the edge of the city for more tiles. One day's shopping list, dictated by Kathy in a phone call toward the final days of construction, included two cement posts to secure the gate, one pair of heavy-duty gloves to replace the ones that had gone missing, more tiles to finish the urinals, one more bathroom sink, a toilet and taps for the staff bathroom (all from different stores). Also on my list were plants for the front garden, wooden poles and brackets for a wall hanging and a laminating machine for the library cards. "And when you have time, please look for a good second-hand car."

More instructions from Kathy trickled in almost daily. She had learned that the outside gutter was blocked so it should be cleaned before it bred mosquitoes. Check the railings to make sure they are safe and tell the night watchman I will pay him a bonus if nothing disappears.

A final request, this one from the workmen scribbled on the back of an envelope and marked URGENT: please buy two live goats so we can celebrate the completion of the project—Ghanaian style.

When the floor tiles were finally dry, I hired a truck to pick up all the furniture from the carpenter—250 chairs, 25 round tables and a dozen large shelves for the upstairs study hall plus 100 stools and chairs for the downstairs theatre.

Kathy arrived a few days before the opening to find the men still working flat out to complete the final details. When the work was almost finished, they put down their tools and retreated to the back of the building where they slaughtered the two goats, cooked the meat over a charcoal fire and enjoyed a celebratory feast.

Only Raymond Sewavi, Kathy's laid-back tiler, chose to work to his own schedule. The afternoon before commissioning day, he took it upon himself to create, with tiles, a Canadian and Ghanaian flag on the floor of the entranceway. This was a nice touch but it was soon clear that he was running out of time. As the day wore on, he was still chipping away trying to perfect the maple leaf on the Canadian flag. Undaunted, he continued well into the night, working by flickering candle light when the power failed, until he finally finished his masterpiece. Kathy and I were there to witness the final touches and we both heaved a huge sigh of relief. It was pitch dark when we returned to the guesthouse to catch a few hours' sleep before the big day.

NOVEMBER 18, 2006, WAS AN AUSPICIOUS DAY FOR THE COMMUNITY of Nima. By 10 a.m., the sun was already beating down on the canopies that sheltered more than 200 assembled guests who gathered for the commissioning of the new Nima Maamobi Community Learning Centre, Kathy's biggest project yet and one that would point her in a whole new direction. There were government officials and village elders, local chiefs and community members, staff and children from the OCLF libraries and a cluster of visitors from Canada.

It was easy to see that something special was happening. Dozens of poker-faced security men hovered about the property, looking a little uncertain of their mission. It turned out that Kathy had been determined to make this day a big splash so she had invited then president of Ghana, John Kufour, to officially open the new building and was told that he had agreed to attend. He was expected to turn up at 10 a.m. Ten o'clock arrived but there was no sign of the president. Time passed, the gathering was growing restless and by 11.30 a.m., there was still no president. So Kathy decided, for the sake of the wilting guests, to begin without him.

The ceremony finally unfolded with much pomp and ceremony. There were words of welcome from the local chiefs and elders, a greeting from Canadian High Commissioner, Lucy Edwards, and speeches from various local officials. The Nima Library choir sang and children from the Nungua Library danced. Richard Larbi, a student from the School for the Blind, read a poem and Mariam, a long-time literacy student, welcomed guests.

The ceremony continued with children from the Kathy Knowles Community Library stepping forward. They stood rigidly at attention, each one holding up a flag of Ghana as they earnestly sang Ghana's national anthem.

"God bless our homeland, Ghana,
And make our nation great and strong
Bold to defend forever
The cause of freedom and of right."

Then, with barely a pause, they switched hands and thrust a red and white Canadian flag into the air while belting out a spirited rendition of O *Canada*, Canada's national anthem.

The children scampered back to their seats and Florence Adjepong, one of the OCLF directors, stepped up to the podium. "Kathy has redefined the concept of community libraries," she told the audience. "They're not just rooms that house books, but they are places where people—men, women and children—are transformed, where illiterate women learn to read, where petty traders or seamstresses find a new confidence, self-esteem, and the voice of participation. They are places where children develop their reading habits, acquire favourite authors, learn new skills, and unearth hidden talents. Kathy, you deserve an award for the impact you have had on the lives of all of us here. For this, we say thank you. Ayekoo! God bless you."

The ceremony was nearing the end and the president had still not turned up so Kathy continued to improvise. She began by thanking all the guests for helping to launch the new facility. Waving her arm towards the new structure, she told them "This is YOUR building. It is here for you, the people of Nima, to use and enjoy."

Next, she invited all her workmen to join her on the podium. Up stepped Bright, her loyal mason, who looked shy and uncomfortable to be singled out. Then she introduced Theophilus, her painter "who knows more than anyone what a good paint job looks like." Next was Raymond, her tiler, and finally, Edward Modzakah, her 72-year-old carpenter. It is he who has crafted by hand and without electricity in his modest workshop all the furniture in all her libraries. "None of this would have been possible without the hard work and dedication of these amazing men," she said. "This beautiful building is their creation." Loud applause while the men shifted nervously from foot to foot, uncertain where to look. Rarely had they received such praise.

Kathy then explained to the guests that, since the president had still not arrived, she had decided to invite "my good friend, the carpenter" to officially open the new building. There were a few puzzled glances over this breach of protocol as 'Mr. Carpenter,' beaming like a young schoolboy, led a parade of guests over to the new building, plucked the decorated scissors from a silver tray, and snipped the ribbon, declaring the building officially open. At once, the invited guests elbowed their way through every door to see what lay inside.

The first group moved upstairs where they found a study space with seating for 150 students. Behind a circular counter were shelves of school texts and reference books and a supply of daily newspapers and magazines. The upper floor is the realm of the older students, many of whom live in crowded rooms and often must study by candlelight. Here, they can work in clean, well-lit surroundings. Downstairs, a curved stage provides a setting for drama, dancing and cultural activities that would become one of Kathy's most far-reaching projects.

As in all her libraries, it is the garden that is Kathy's pride and joy. Even before the sod was turned for the new building, she had arranged to have dozens of bougainvillaea seedlings planted around the property and four flowering trees to honour special donors and departed friends. Ghana's tropical sun and rains will ensure that the trees will soon be large enough to provide shade for the long meandering Gaudi bench which provides ample space for relaxation.

To this day, no one, including the A.M.A. who delivered the invitation to the president, could explain his absence. Nonetheless, Kathy was happy with the way things unfolded. When all the guests had left and the staff were packing up the canopies and cleaning up the litter, she climbed upstairs to the terrace, sank into a chair and heaved a sigh of relief. It had been almost six full years since she made that first phone call to get this project off the ground—six years of fundraising in Canada, wrangling with bureaucrats in Ghana, and working with planners and contractors on both sides of the Atlantic. Yes, she was exhausted, but as she looked out over the rooftops of Nima, any doubts she once had about this huge project vanished.

ONCE THE NEW FACILITY WAS OFFICIALLY OPEN, THE NEXT CHALLENGE was the hiring of staff to run the library. The Accra Municipal Assembly (A.M.A.) ran an open competition and selected six staff members plus a director, Abdul Moro Taufic. Taufic had grown up in Nima and was one of the fortunate few who not only was able to finish school but managed to graduate from the University of Ghana with a diploma. He was pleased to accept the position of director of the new centre and welcomed the opportunity to help his community and give its people the same chance he had received.

The vision that had driven Kathy for six long years was not without its disappointments. One involved the payment of staff salaries. Long before the centre opened, the A.M.A. had guaranteed in writing to pay the water and electricity bills and all the staff salaries. However, the building opened in November 2006 but the staff did not receive their first pay cheque until the following September. Kathy was able to partially advance these salaries and amazingly, the ever-patient staff managed to keep the place going.

Kathy uses every visit to Ghana to press the A.M.A. into more action on the salary front. One trip after another often leads to promises but no action. "We don't have any money," the official would answer. Kathy would bite her lip to conceal her anger. "But here is the agreement," she would say, waving the signed document. "We have done our part. You MUST find the money." Her exasperation often reached boiling point but somehow she managed to control her disappointment. "We always want our libraries to be self-sustaining so that if I was to fall off the edge of the earth tomorrow, they would continue. But I keep running into these impossible road blocks."

Kathy acknowledges that her meetings with the authorities are the toughest part of her work in Ghana. The challenge of getting staff salaries paid is matched only by facing stubborn officials who show little sympathy when the power fails or the water is cut off when the bill has not been paid. This too often requires letters to various departments, plus phone calls and endless visits. On a recent trip, she was asked to pick up a cheque for a payment owing to her. This took three visits on three successive days since the cheque required three different signatures and each signee "has just left the office." "These tasks are so time-consuming but it is important to insist that the government meets its share of responsibilities. So I just keep pushing," she says.

A couple of years ago, when she turned up at the A.M.A. office to press forward her case once again, one official greeted her by saying "Oh yes. I remember now. You're the troublemaker!" But she is determined to stick to her principles. "I see my time in Ghana very much as a journey of faith. All the obstacles we face are now part-and-parcel of what we expect but it is still so often a struggle." Nevertheless, in spite of the many setbacks she encounters on each visit, her optimism rarely wavers. "We are moving forward," she says, even after the most difficult day, as she tries hard to convince those around her as well as herself. Fortunately, this is slowly changing. During her visit in August 2012, it was evident that government support for her libraries is inching ahead. Earlier that year, they came up with a small salary increase for all staff members.

DESPITE SET-BACKS AND INCESSANT WRANGLING WITH THE A.M.A., THE new Learning Centre quickly took on a life of its own and has spawned many far-reaching activities. The study space upstairs is well patronized from 9 a.m. until 9 p.m. Monday to Friday and until 5 p.m. on Saturday. Downstairs, an increasing number of adults attend evening literacy classes four evenings a week while the ever-popular theatre and dance groups meet to practise and perform. Says Director Taufic: "We want this place to become the nerve-centre for the community of Nima, to be the source of change and a focal point for community groups. Already, many groups use the facility and we hope this will continue to grow. Insh'Allah (with God's help)."

Kathy and her family in the garden on Osu Avenue. *(FROM L TO R: Sophie, Kathy, Alastair, Kaitlan, John and Akosua.)* The flamboyant tree behind was the setting for her first reading circle.

Kathy welcoming children to her garden library, 1991.

The arrival of the shipping container that would become the Osu Library, later called the Kathy Knowles Community Library, 1992.

Kathy Knowles Community Library today, transformed from a 40 foot shipping container.

The interior of the eight foot wide Kathy Knowles Community Library. *PHOTO CREDIT: Alex Baum*

Kathy reading to children at the Osu Library, 2005.

Winnipeg volunteers after packing the first shipping container of books in 2006.

The Osu Library's annual Sponsored Walk raises funds for the library.

The Nima Maamobi Gale Community Library, once a dilapidated building on a dusty terrain, is now a handsome structure surrounded by flowering shrubs and trees.

*PHOTO CREDIT: Bill Lee.*

Michaëlle Jean, Canada's 27th Governor General, on a visit to the Nima Library in 2006.

*PHOTO CREDIT: Sgt. Eric Jolin, Rideau Hall*

The Nima Maamobi Learning Centre, located directly behind the Nima Library, 2007.

The Kathy Knowles Theatre Company dancers performing at the Nima Maamobi Community Learning Centre, 2008.

Kathy with Masawoud Zakari soon after a major operation allowed him to walk for the first time, 2007.

Joanna reading "My Red Book" to her library children. The book is one of more than 35 children's books published by the Osu Children's Library Fund.

The opening in 2008 of the Kathy Knowles Community Library in Goi, a small fishing village east of Accra. The sign, like those on all OCLF libraries, was created and donated by Canadian ceramic artist, Mimi Cabri.

Deborah reading to children at the Mamprobi Gale Community Library, 2012.

The ground floor of the Nungua Community Library is packed with keen readers every day.

Kathy checking plans with contractor Kojo Maclean for the Accra College of Education Community Library, 2010.

Kathy's loyal carpenter, Edward Modzakah, making chairs for the new library, 2010.

The Accra College of Education Community Library opened in 2011.

OCLF's two Ghanaian board members, Emma Amoo-Gottfried (left) and Florence Adjepong (right), both heads of large private schools, whose children attended Kathy's first library in the garden.

## CHAPTER 11

# A Theatre for Nima

WHEN KATHY AND ROGER WERE DESIGNING THE NEW LEARNING CENTRE, their plan from the start was to include space for theatre productions and cultural dancing. They allocated the ground floor of the building for this purpose and included a semi-circular stage and seating for an audience of 250.

There was already a small but keen group of library members who had shown impressive acting ability. This group goes back to 1998 when, as members of the smaller Nima Library, they wrote and performed short skits for special occasions. To do so in such a cramped space, they had to shove back the bookshelves and storage cabinets and move between the tables and stools. It was a modest beginning but their enthusiasm and obvious talent convinced Kathy that she should include a proper stage in her plans for the new building.

The day the Nima Centre opened its doors, the fledgling actors were thrilled to see the new performance space. They wasted no time in gathering more friends who ranged in age and background. Some had never been to school, others spoke only basic English. But they were eager and willing to learn and before long and with repeated rehearsals, they were all participating in the early plays.

That group of about 30 met regularly to discuss their plans. To start, they decided to name themselves the Kathy Knowles Theatre Company Limited. The person they chose to be director of the company was Martin Adjei Legend.

Martin is a shy and serious young man who was born in 1984 in the North of Ghana He lost both his parents before he was eight and, at 14, relatives sent him down to Accra to live with two older brothers in Nima.

His brothers helped him complete junior high school but they were unwilling to pay his fees to enter senior high school. One day, he happened to pass by the Nima Library and was drawn in by their free noontime lunches. "Things were very bad at home so these really saved me," he recalls.

Martin was on the verge of dropping out of school when he was visiting the library and met Kathy. She talked with him for a long time and felt that he was a bright lad and deserved to return to school. With Hannah's agreement, she gave him one of the first scholarships to cover his school fees and he enrolled at once in St. Frances Senior Secondary School.

It was at high school that Martin came under the spell of literature and theatre. He and some friends formed a small theatre group and they wrote and performed their own plays. When the Learning Centre opened, Martin was among the first to step forward and organize the theatre company. He remembers being "very humbled" when the group chose him to be the director of their new company. "They gave me the courage and the support to handle this responsibility," he said in typical modesty.

The next year, Martin directed his first play. It was *The Gods are Not to Blame*, an adaptation of the classic Greek story of Oedipus Rex, by Nigerian author Ola Rotimi. It seemed the whole community of Nima, adults and children, turned up for that first performance. Most had never seen a play but their curiosity drew them in and they packed the hall.

Kathy was so impressed by the obvious commitment of the group and the positive response from the audience that OCLF obtained a grant from Alberta's Wild Rose Foundation that enabled Calgary theatre director, Eric Rose and his wife Caitlin Gallichan-Lowe, a drama teacher, to travel to Ghana for two weeks in the summer of 2008 to coach the new company and help the actors develop their theatre skills. They ran drama workshops where the students worked on writing and producing plays on subjects that touched their lives. They also organized a week-long drama camp for 20 children from four of the OCLF libraries. The youngsters ate, slept and played together as they explored different theatrical ideas—masks, clowns, movement, lights and scenery—all the details involved in putting on a play. At week's end, they produced a short play, *The Name of the Tree*, an African folk tale by Celia Barker Lottridge. The children wore plaster masks they had made, acted out characters they had developed and performed a story they loved.

Sterling Lee, an American Peace Corps volunteer, was watching the play that night. She had spent two years working at a school near one of the OCLF libraries so she knew many of the children. At the end of the play, she went backstage to greet the actors. "Those kids were so excited, like children on a sugar high without the sugar," she said. "They were all hugging each other and exchanging addresses. One little girl I knew who was always very quiet at school was talking and laughing and dancing with so much confidence. Another was crying so hard because she didn't want to leave. I almost started crying myself when I saw what a huge impact this program had on those kids."

Eric's influence on the theatre company was huge. He also proved to be an important mentor to Martin who blossomed under his tutelage and managed to take his first bold steps at theatre directing. At the end of the session, he and Eric co-directed a production of *The Legend of Aku Sika*, a play by Ghanaian playwright, Martin Owusu, inspired by his own personal experience bringing up a handicapped son. Eric called it "a powerful play that challenges our preconceptions and prejudices against people who are deformed or disabled."

Martin Owusu is not only a leading Ghanaian playwright but a professor of drama at the University of Ghana. He attended the performance of his play in Nima and was so moved by the quality of the acting that he invited the troupe to perform in his theatre at the university. "It was an amazing opportunity for those kids," said Kathy. "To act in a big professional theatre with sophisticated lighting and a large audience just blew their minds. When they told me about it afterwards, they had tears in their eyes just recounting the experience. 'Just think,' one of them said 'here we were, a bunch of kids from Nima, and we were performing at the University of Ghana!'"

In the audience that night was Deborah Ahenkorah, a Ghanaian who, as a child, was an early visitor to Kathy's first library. "I was blown away by watching those kids," she said. "There is still a lot of class separation in Ghana and people look at Nima as a dirty place where nothing positive could ever happen. But look what those kids have done! They are not on drugs or on the street doing God-knows-what. They are on stage acting out the most amazing play."

WHEN KATHY SET OUT ON THAT MORNING RUN IN WINNIPEG SIX YEARS earlier, she could never have imagined that this new building would provide the impetus for such a creative and far-reaching venture. The group continued to put on plays and even made a start at writing their own works "to bring people's attention to some of the evils of our society" such as abortion, teenage pregnancy, Internet fraud. They even tackled the subject of HIV-AIDS, always an ever-present threat although, according to the AIDS Commission, the disease still only affects 1.9 percent of the Ghanaian population.

Eric and Caitlin returned to Ghana the following summer. Caitlin travelled to the OCLF libraries in Goi and Nungua helping to nurture groups of fledgling actors while Eric worked with the group at the Nima Centre. On his third trip, he brought Tyler Sainsbury, a talented set designer who taught the company about set changes and how to create costumes with limited resources. At the end of their stay, the company performed *The Forbidden Sacrifice*, one of Martin Legend's first plays. It is about a boy who is killed for allegedly killing another. His death brings calamity on the land because he was innocent. The company has performed the play at least a dozen times and theatre groups at six different schools in Accra have also produced the work.

ERIC ROSE'S VISITS TO GHANA WERE TRANSFORMATIVE FOR MANY IN the theatre company, none more than Martin. "Eric's impact on my life is enormous," he told me as we sat one evening in front of the theatre he has come to call his 'home.' "He gave me and every member of the company the confidence to create such beautiful things on stage."

Martin has gone from strength to strength, not only producing plays but writing many of them himself. He has so far written 17 full-length works and has produced half that number, some of which are now being performed in schools around Accra. In September 2011, Michael Williams, director of the Cape Town (South Africa) Opera Company was visiting Ghana and seized the chance to see one of Martin's plays performed by his company. It is called *The Lost Treasure* and is about an old man who scorns the generation that has abandoned the values of the past. On his return to South Africa, Michael wrote: "I really enjoyed your play and the beautiful way you spoke to many of the problems facing Ghana. I loved the main character and was amazed at how word-perfect he was...Your team has real potential, Martin, and you are doing a great job in inspiring them. I can see the hand of a good strong director in your work."

Martin continues to turn out high-quality plays that are winning a wider audience each year. "I have grown to a certain level and am so inspired that I feel there is nothing I cannot write," he says. On the basis of his laudable record as writer, producer and company director, Kathy helped Martin apply for a grant from the Manitoba Council of International Cooperation. His proposal was titled "Theatre: An Essential Tool for Human and Community Development." The grant they received is allowing Martin to tour two of his plays, both addressing social issues, to hold workshops in schools and communities around the country and to upgrade their sound and lighting equipment.

Martin speaks often about the satisfaction he receives not only from helping those in his company grow and mature but also from the fact that he is, in his small way, able to make an impact on the world. "I have been given so much and I am blessed to have a means to give back a little," he said. "My goal is to help close the gap between rich and poor so even the poorest can aspire to be president."

The Kathy Knowles Theatre Company has continued to grow beyond anyone's dreams. In addition to their senior company of more than 30 players, they have formed a second company of 40 junior members. In the summer of 2009, they joined seven other theatre companies in Accra to launch a city-wide Theatre Festival which ran for two months. And in

August 2012, they organized their third all-day Library Theatre Festival which brought together participants from all seven OCLF libraries.

Meanwhile, those in the company are proud of what they have become. They are proud too that they are changing the face of Nima. And much of the credit goes to Martin. "It is only by the grace of God—and even more by Kathy Knowles—that I am what I am today. She took me and set me straight. That is why I am trying to do the same for others."

IT WAS IN DECEMBER 2009 THAT THE KATHY KNOWLES THEATRE Company embarked on its most challenging work, an African opera called *The Orphans of Qumbu* by South African composer Michael Williams.

The opera came about when Kathy learned that her daughter Sophie, a music graduate from York University in Toronto, would be joining her in Ghana. She was looking for a project for Sophie to tackle and found on the web a work she saw as a perfect fit. Opera was a totally new concept for most Ghanaians, especially those living in Nima, but the company was willing to try.

Sophie and Martin auditioned dozens of children and selected a cast of 35 aspiring young opera stars. That was their first challenge since few of them knew how to sing. An even bigger hurdle was that, at her first rehearsal, when Sophie handed out the sheet music, she discovered that not one of the participants had seen a music score before and several in the group were unable to read the English text.

There were many glitches, of course, not least of which was the lead female singer dropping out at the last minute. Sophie was undaunted and jumped in and sang the part. Somehow, the show came together in just six short weeks, thanks largely to the skill and patience of Sophie. "When we finally finished staging the last part and singing the last song," she recalled, "I was overcome by the amazing feeling that comes from being part of a cast that has worked hard, grown so much and together, created a great piece." Their efforts culminated in three packed performances with standing ovations every night. The local assemblyman from Nima was among the honoured guests. He watched the entire production and wept at the final curtain.

It was a heroic accomplishment for Sophie who directed the music and for Martin who stage-managed the performance. Kathy was deservedly proud. "It wasn't so much the quality of performance that we were aiming for. What was more important was the fact that all those kids gained confidence, learned to work together and many of them surprised themselves by learning to sing." Martin later wrote a letter of thanks to Kathy telling her that his company was delighted to be the first to introduce an opera to their community. It was another example of Kathy's instinctive talent for hatching new ideas and following them through with unwavering faith and conviction.

IT HAS BEEN A LONG JOURNEY MAKING THE NEW CENTRE HAPPEN AND Kathy is immensely proud of it. In its short life, it has won rave reviews from both the local community and from all its visitors. The former mayor of Accra stopped by before the opening and was effusive in his praise. "It is so-o-o beautiful," he told Kathy, planting his arm around her shoulder, then added "You know, this building could change the face of Nima." It was a prophetic statement that would soon come true.

## CHAPTER 12

# A Distinguished Visitor recalls Ghana's Troubled Past

THE EUPHORIA OF THE CENTRE'S OPENING HAD BARELY WANED WHEN another event, a week later, brought great excitement to the whole Nima community. This was a visit from Canada's then governor general, Michaëlle Jean. Mme. Jean had been named governor general of Canada in September 2005 and she chose to visit Ghana as part of her first pan-African state visit the following year. She had one overriding reason for making this choice: she was an immigrant from the Caribbean island of Haiti and she wished to honour her ancestors who left Africa as slaves and were piled aboard rickety cargo ships that carried them across the sea to the New World.

Mme. Jean was born in Port-au-Prince, Haiti's capital. She and her family fled to Canada in 1968 when she was just 11 as violence escalated under Haiti's brutal dictator, Francois Duvalier, known as 'Papa Doc.' The family settled in Montreal.

Mme. Jean excelled at school, completed university in Montreal and, in the 1980s, became a popular host of national television news programs.

Children have always been close to Michaëlle Jean's heart. Relatively late in life, she and her husband adopted Marie-Eden, an orphaned baby from Haiti. It was not surprising, therefore, that when she was planning her trip to Ghana, she made a special request to visit a children's library. The Nima Library was her personal choice.

The day before the planned visit, an advance team of nine, most of them security scouts, arrived in long black vehicles to check out the location and the buildings. When they drove out of the parking lot, the lead car hit a rock and scraped its undercarriage. The rattled driver then turned out onto the Kanda Highway—the wrong way onto a one-way street! It was a dramatic introduction to the vice-regal visit.

The next day, things unfolded according to plan. The governor general's sleek black limousine drew up in front of the library right on time and the whole community gathered around to watch as Mme. Jean climbed out of the car. Kathy stepped forward to welcome her and placing her arm around the governor general's shoulders, steered her over to the library. At the entrance, Mme. Jean removed her shoes, as per library rules, and entered the room where a dozen children, all wearing spotlessly clean school uniforms, sat nervously waiting.

The governor general greeted all the children, then sat down in a corner, picked up a book and read them a story. She began with *Fati and the Honey Tree*, one of the children's favourites. "Fati was a little girl who ran like the wind, who loved to laugh, and who always tried hard to do as she was told." The children sat entranced.

Mme. Jean then read another book about snow which prompted many questions. "How do you gather the snow and pack it to make a snowball," asked one child. "She taught us that Canada is located in North America," said another. More questions followed before it was all over. The governor general handed Hannah a box of children's books, slipped her shoes back on and waved goodbye to all the delighted youngsters.

Mme. Jean then moved next door to the new centre where she met with a group of Canadian volunteers working on literacy projects in Ghana. At the close of the discussion, she signalled to the new staff members who stood nervously huddled in a distant corner. They had been on the job barely two weeks and were uncertain how they should act. They needn't have worried. She spoke to each one individually, then gathered them together for a group photograph.

That visit made such a big impression on the staff and children that many of them sent the governor general letters of thanks. There was some confusion about her title: one child addressed her as 'Dear Mrs. Governor' while another wrote 'Dear Ms. General Governor.' There was even one who came up with the title 'Dear General.'

When Michaëlle Jean returned to Canada, she sent Kathy a letter of thanks.

*Dear Kathy,*

*It was a pleasure to meet you and to see the extraordinary work you have done at the Nima Maamobi Community Learning Centre in Accra.*

*As Canadians, it is so important for us to realize the construct-ive influence we can have on the world. You are proof that the vision and actions of just one person can make a tremendous difference in so many lives! It was wonderful to see the eager faces of the children at the library, who all share an infectious enthusiasm for reading. I was delighted to join in their reading circle that afternoon.*

*Thank you so much for sending me the children's letters and photos. They are filled with so much hope, imagination and faith in the goodness of the world. I wish you and all the staff of the library and learning centre every success in future endeavours.*

*—Michaëlle Jean*

The day after her visit to Nima, the governor general flew by heli-copter to Elmina, a dozen kilometres west of Cape Coast, to see where her ancestors had left as slaves for their journey across the sea to Haiti.

There are still many remnants of the slave trade in Ghana in the dozens of forts and castles built along the coast by Europeans between 1482 and 1786. It is hardly surprising, given her heritage, that the gov-ernor general had asked specially to visit one of these sites and had de-cided on St. George's Castle in Elmina which had been one of the first and largest hubs of the slave trade.

The forts and castles that dot the coast of Ghana were originally built as trading posts for the Europeans who saw the riches, primarily gold, that lay under the soil of what was then called the Gold Coast. The Portuguese were the first to arrive and initially, they traded in gold, ivory and pepper. Trade flourished so, in 1482, they built St. George's Castle as their first permanent trading post. Word spread quickly and the coastal region of Ghana became a busy destination for merchants and traders.

It was in the early 16th century that the Europeans began opening plantations in the New World. Suddenly, there was a huge demand for cheap labour to work on these plantations so they looked to Africa. Portugal led the way, then the British, French, and Dutch followed. The Danes and Germans joined later in the scramble for African humans. They landed all along the coast of West Africa but a high proportion of them headed to what was then the Gold Coast, now Ghana.

They arrived in ships loaded with manufactured goods to barter or trade for slaves. This marked the beginning of the slave trade, one of the most shameful periods in history.

The slaves that were captured from villages all over the country were made to walk hundreds of kilometres chained to each other with iron shackles. They were only allowed to rest occasionally at a transit camp before moving on to the 'slave castles'—those in Elmina and Cape Coast were the largest—where as many as 200 slaves would be packed into one room. There, their new masters branded them with the insignia of their owners, herded them through the long passageways and shoved them onto waiting ships for the two-month journey, mostly to the New World. The late Philip Curtin, an authority on the African slave trade, estimated that more than nine million men, women and children were shipped from West Africa to North and South America, most of them between 1701 and 1870. It is believed that as many as 5,000 slaves a year left from the Gold Coast alone.

When the governor general stepped inside the castle walls, trailing an entourage of Canadian and Ghanaian officials, she paused in the cell that had once housed the female slaves. She learned from her guide that this was where women were starved and often raped by guards or soldiers. She then moved on to the castle's clammy dungeon and saw where the slaves were led to the waiting boats. "I stood at the 'Gate of No Return' and thought of my own ancestors who were captured and enslaved here," she said later. "I prayed for those who had passed through that door and I prayed for those who never made it to those faraway lands.

"As I stood there, I could hear the voices of children playing and laughing. I know that there are still children today who are enslaved. I know that slavery is still a reality. We should never forget nor should we ever feel indifferent to those realities."

The governor general accepted a spray of pink flowers which she placed at the barred gate. As she took one last look at the waters that carried her ancestors across the sea, she said: "I think there is a time for tears and a time for silence. Then there comes a time for celebration and a time to appreciate the meaning of freedom."

As she was leaving St. George's Castle, Mme. Jean passed through an archway that bore the words:

IN EVERLASTING MEMORY OF THE ANGUISH OF OUR ANCESTORS
MAY THOSE WHO DIED REST IN PEACE
MAY THOSE WHO RETURN FIND THEIR ROOTS
MAY HUMANITY NEVER AGAIN PERPETUATE
SUCH INJUSTICE AGAINST HUMANITY
WE THE LIVING VOW TO UPHOLD THIS.

MICHAËLLE JEAN'S FIVE-YEAR TERM AS GOVERNOR GENERAL ENDED IN 2010. She was then appointed the United Nations Special Envoy to Haiti where she is helping in the rehabilitation of her homeland following the devastating earthquake in January 2010 that left the country in ruins. More recently, she was also named chancellor of the University of Ottawa.

## CHAPTER 13

# In Praise of African Women

WOMEN IN GHANA, AS IN MUCH OF AFRICA, STILL MAKE UP THE LARGEST proportion of those living below the poverty line. They are born and bred to look after their children, to do the shopping, the cooking—all the duties needed to provide for the family. They are also brought up to respect and serve their husband and male relatives.

Their daughters grow up with the same expectations. Unlike their brothers, it is they who are often kept at home to help with the younger siblings, to fetch the water or to carry out the household duties. In rural areas, they are also expected to help on the farm.

Not surprisingly, a high proportion of the girls who attend school drop out before they complete high school. As a result, they rarely break out of the grinding cycle of poverty. A study by the South African-based ActionAid International found that the public expectation of a girl's education is much lower than that of boys. The required household chores and early pregnancy are factors that have contributed to the dropout rate among girls. The study also noted that at the tertiary education level (post high school), boys outnumber girls three to one.

Gender issues still remain deeply entrenched in Ghana as they do elsewhere on the continent. Gender-based violence (spousal abuse) is also still a wide-spread reality in many regions of the country. So too is the shame on a woman's family if she is unable to produce a child. One man, whose daughter had just undergone her *ninth* miscarriage, told me that, while he showed concern for his daughter's physical and emotional health, the worst part was the shame it brought to his family. She will likely lose her husband, her livelihood, her self-esteem, and would never be acceptable to another man.

Some girls, who represent a small percentage of the population, have had the good fortune to be born into an upper-class family and thus manage to avoid some of these challenges. They can benefit from a good education at a top private school and graduate with greater opportunities. It is they who are able to become doctors, lawyers and educators. Even so, the sad reality is that even they rarely reach the top ranks, especially in male-dominated professions. According to Sarah Akrofi-Quarcoo, lecturer at the School of Communication Studies at the University of Ghana, only a very few women have reached decision-making positions in the many media houses around the country. "In the over 200 radio stations, more than 130 newspapers and 30 authorized TV stations in Ghana, only a small handful of women are top editors," she told me. "Furthermore, only one radio station and one newspaper are owned by women."

The political scene isn't much better. Before the December 2012 election, women occupied only 19 out of the 230 seats in the national parliament—a scant 8.3 percent—and only 11 percent of them were in ministerial positions. There was little change following that election when 29 women, just 11 percent, were elected to the 275 seat house. "Since the country adopted a democratic system of governance in the early 1990s," Akrofi-Quarcoo adds, "various women's groups have been fighting for increased women's representation in public life and in politics. So far, they have made little progress."

WOMEN WHO DO NOT HAVE THE CHANCE TO FURTHER THEIR EDUCAtion and climb up the ladder into decision-making roles can occasionally move ahead, through sheer determination and extremely hard work, coupled with a dash of good luck. Joanna Felih is a shining example.

Joanna had the good fortune to knock on the Knowles' door back in 1991 looking for work and was hired by Kathy to be her part-time housekeeper. She proved to be such a conscientious worker and a quick and eager learner that Kathy put her in charge of her first permanent library in their garden. Several years later, she was placed on the government payroll and, though her pay is still pitifully small, she is guaranteed a salary until her retirement at 60 and a small pension after that. Thanks to her hard work and dedication, she has clearly put the Osu Library firmly on the map. Though its official name has long since been the Kathy Knowles Community Library, Joanna's presence has always been so important that it is more often referred to as 'Joanna's library.'

"Joanna is quite simply a marvel," Kathy says. "If someone came to me with a PhD in Library Science, I wouldn't trade Joanna for them. She is totally responsible, works very hard and has rarely missed a day in all the time she has been with us.

"I think what feeds her is the very positive reaction from the children and their parents. That keeps her going." A bulging filing cabinet in a corner of Joanna's office contains dozens of letters from children, their parents and community leaders all attesting to the role that she and the library have played in their lives.

Joanna is a beautiful woman with an open face, a benevolent smile and a husky, joyful laugh that erupts at any opportunity. Thanks to her dedication to the children she serves, her library has become the real hub of all the OCLF operations in Ghana. It may be small in size but it is large in spirit and it sits like a benign auntie watching over its younger offspring.

There is no doubt that the strength of all OCLF libraries lies in their many fine librarians. At present, all the head librarians are women (the one male has left to pursue his studies) and of the 40 government-paid staff members, 24 of them—more than half—are women. They are all doing exemplary work to make their own facilities what they are today. But it is Joanna who stands out as the mother figure overseeing the activities in the growing network of libraries.

When anyone enters her library, she offers them a warm *Akwaaba*. It could a child paying his first-ever visit to the library, a parent who is anxious to know what happens in this now-famous building or a curious tourist who has read about the library in the Bradt Guide to Ghana (5th edition). Joanna's voice exudes care and compassion, and her sentences are punctuated with a throaty 'Yoo,' meaning 'Okay' or 'you are right' in her native Ewe (ay-way) language.

Joanna's career as a full-time librarian took off the day the Osu Library opened its doors in November 1992. Kathy had full confidence in Joanna, entrusting her to run the new building and Joanna relished this opportunity. After the Knowles family left Ghana, she moved to a room she rented far from the library. She lived there alone caring for her new baby, Jennifer, though she was fortunate to have the moral and financial support of a caring husband, Bless, who lived and worked at a government job hours away.

Like thousands of Ghanaian women, Joanna faced many hardships. Her day started well before dawn when she would strap baby Jennifer on her back and set out on three different trips to fetch three 40 pound buckets of water from the communal tap, enough for their bathing and cooking needs. Then she would travel one and a half hours by tro-tro to the library, again with her baby cradled on her back. She would work the whole day at the library then take the same long journey home. Says Kathy: "Given all that, I never once heard her complain. Not once."

JOANNA'S STORY IS TYPICAL OF COUNTLESS WOMEN IN GHANA, AND elsewhere in Africa, who must work double time to make ends meet and to provide a better life for their children. She was born in 1967 in Avee, then a small village of barely 1,000 in the Volta Region. Her father had died of a stroke in the early 1970s when she and her six siblings were still in school so the children grew up helping their mother grow vegetables and sell them in the village market.

UNESCO estimates that, in developing countries such as Ghana, 12 to 18 hours of a woman's day are spent preparing meals, caring for children, gathering water and collecting firewood. It was no different in Joanna's family. As she moved into her teens, she dropped out of secondary school so she could help support the family. Since job prospects in Avee were bleak, she decided, at 23, to leave her village and travel to Accra where her older sister had found work. It was through her sister that she learned about the position with the Knowles family.

Step into Joanna's library any time of day and she will be there, welcoming children by the dozens. She knows them all by name, follows their progress in school and is always watching for signs of trouble there or at home. As the children arrive, she steers them to the water basin to wash their hands, reminds them to remove their shoes before stepping into the library, then helps them choose an appropriate book or a game. Somehow, she manages to keep order in a room packed with excited children—an exceptional feat given that the room is less than eight feet wide.

In mid-afternoon, she gathers everyone inside where they squat on floor mats for story time. Story time is sacrosanct in all Kathy's libraries and this one is no exception. When the children are quietly seated, Joanna pulls up a stool, opens a book and holds it up so they can all see the pictures. Then she starts to read. "*Once upon a time...*" and a chorus of young voices repeats "*time, time,*" and she continues the story. Says Kathy: "It is Joanna's passion for what she does that has allowed us to move forward so quickly. She is just so gifted with those children."

Joanna's job as head librarian also involves supervising staff, helping with literacy classes, developing programs—music, cultural dancing, crafts are all popular activities. When Kathy is in Canada, she keeps an eye on all the other libraries and pays regular visits to each one to deal with any problems that arise. She has learned to manage most of the complex banking issues for the project and is the resident trainer for lay librarians—at least half a dozen annually—who come from around the country for her two-week training course to learn the different aspects of setting up and running a library.

JOANNA ALSO ACTS AS CUSTODIAN OF THE SMALL GUESTHOUSE THAT the organization rents on the edge of Nima. She lives there with her daughter Jennifer and is a caring 'den-mother' for the volunteers who travel to Ghana to help in the libraries. To run the guesthouse, with its constant comings and goings, would challenge most people but Joanna takes it all in her stride. She starts her day at 5 a.m., sweeps the compound, often prepares breakfast for as many as five hungry bodies (fresh orange juice, home-made muffins and French toast are her specialties) and still has time to make a head start on the evening meal.

She reaches the library by 9 a.m., and spends most of the day there, oblivious to the noise of so many hyper children or of the intense heat of the African sun.

The library closes at 5 p.m. She walks several blocks to catch a tro-tro for the trip home, stopping first at the local market to pick up supplies for dinner. When there is a special price on oranges, she returns to the market, fills a 50 pound sack to the brim, boosts it onto her head, and walks back along the crowded sidewalk, and down a dozen steep cement steps (no railings) into the guesthouse. "If you grow up carrying your baby on your back and a gallon of water on your head, a sack of oranges is nothing," she says. "We are strong, strong."

Joanna is home for only minutes before she begins peeling and chopping vegetables for the evening meal. If there is electricity, she uses the stove. When the electricity fails (the local term is 'light off'), she barely flinches as she lights a candle, presses it onto a tin lid, switches on a kerosene burner on the floor and continues her meal preparations.

She cooks everything from scratch. Dinner is usually a Ghanaian specialty such as groundnut (peanut) soup, a stew of chicken and tomatoes liberally laced with peanut butter, or 'red red,' a bean stew served with fried plantains. To celebrate a special occasion, she moves into the outside courtyard, stands firmly beside a large bowl and pounds cassava into a pulp with a six foot tall pestle to prepare *fufu,* a popular Ghanaian dish that looks like a gooey ball of dough and is dipped into a tomato-based stew. Under Joanna's tutelage, you dig out a wad with your right hand, mush it around in the sauce and pop it in your mouth. No cutlery is allowed for this meal. Just fingers. If there is no power, dinner is by candlelight or by a flashlight propped up on the table. Joanna, like most Ghanaians, is unruffled by the frequent electricity outages. "The lights will return," she asserts with confidence. They do, eventually. By 9 p.m., she foregoes the nearby bed, unrolls her mat and stretches out on the floor. She is more than ready to sleep.

Joanna's busy week barely lets up on the weekend. She does several piles of laundry, all by hand and often for as many as five people. Ghanaians are meticulous about cleanliness, scrubbing themselves in a morning and evening bath. Joanna is no exception.

Sunday brings a welcome break in her life. Like many people in Ghana, Joanna has grown up with a deep Christian faith. She attends St. Kizito's Roman Catholic Church in Nima every Sunday morning setting out before 7 a.m. and dressed like royalty in a colourful tight-fitting sarong-like outfit. Kathy and I have joined her on many occasions and we are always amazed to find the church is always packed to over-flowing with more than 1,500 people squeezed into the main floor and another 500 upstairs on a semi-circular balcony. The minute the choir strikes up, the bongo drums take flight, a string of young priests sway to the music and the whole congregation leaps to its feet, arms waving and hands clapping in time with the music. It is a true celebration.

The service ends and everyone spills out into the front courtyard where as many more parishioners wait to join the second mass of the morning. After the first church visit I made with Joanna, I noticed on the journey home that she sat silently as our taxi nosed its way through the crowded street. Breaking the silence, I asked her what that weekly service means to her and, no doubt, to the more than two-thirds of the congregation who are women. She paused for a minute, then replied. "The women are there because we are the ones with all the problems. We are the ones who need it most."

In spite of the heavy load she is carrying, Joanna never complains or shows an ounce of self-pity. She has had her share of knocks—losing her father at such an early age, helping to care for her widowed mother and younger siblings, working in the fields and carrying water from afar and, more recently, losing her elder sister who died of a stroke at less than 50 years of age.

And now, shouldering much of the responsibility of an NGO based thousands of miles away.

Some would call her a stoic. This was never more apparent than on one occasion when she was returning home in a tro-tro. Suddenly, the engine began to smoke and all the passengers scrambled to get out through the doors. In the crush, Joanna received a very deep gash in her leg. Somehow, she managed to walk home leaving a trail of blood behind her but it was clear she needed medical attention.

I was at the guesthouse when she arrived home looking pale and anxious. We sent Jennifer to a nearby pharmacy to fetch a bandage and some ointment but the store was out of everything. "Come back next week," they told her. We tore up a sheet, wrapped it around her leg and we helped her stagger to the street and hailed a taxi. It was a pitch black night, with 'light off' in the whole area, but she rallied the strength to bargain with the taxi driver for the best price. At the hospital, which was eerily quiet with dark deserted corridors, she was greeted by a sympathetic nurse. A doctor arrived soon after, examined her, cleaned and stitched up the wound and gave her a tetanus shot before sending her home. Throughout it all, she uttered barely a whimper. She was then 41 and it was the first time she had ever been inside a hospital.

## CHAPTER 14

# A Home Away from Home

THE GUESTHOUSE THAT JOANNA MANAGES IS ALSO HOME TO KATHY AND me during our twice-yearly visits to Ghana. The place is simple, just three small rooms backing onto the busy Nima community. Comfortable it is but quiet it is not. The building not only faces the busy Kanda Highway with the honking and screeching of round-the-clock traffic but a pathway behind is the dirt thoroughfare for a never-ending stream of bleating goats and squawking roosters. Above it all are the amplified wails of the muezzins from half a dozen nearby mosques calling the faithful to prayer.

Joanna has managed to turn the guesthouse into a snug home away from home for us both. Kathy, especially, is more than happy living there, close to the community she serves, and she is oblivious to its limited facilities—bucket showers (scooping a cup of water from a pail and sloshing it over your body), intermittent electricity, a temperamental ceiling-fan, and a tightly rationed water supply. There are shrieks of joy when the first drops of water sputter from the tap and even louder shouts of delight when the lights come back on. Uncertain Internet access enables us to keep in touch with family and friends and a tiny transistor radio brings news from afar, thanks to a crackling BBC world service.

From the day she began her work with the libraries, Kathy has chosen to live modestly and to forgo the trappings enjoyed by most expatriates—spacious housing, fancy cars, air-conditioning. She also keeps a much lower profile than the many large NGOs who barely know she exists. "When you are serving people who have so little, I would not feel comfortable living any other way," she says. She groans at even the hint of opulence. "That's ten times more than our staff members are paid in a month." Once, when invited to an expensive Accra restaurant, she was stunned by the size of the portions so asked the waiter for a box, scooped up the leftovers and carried them back for the library's night watchman.

Frugality is Kathy's mantra and it guides her every move. Whenever she takes a commercial taxi, she is a master at bargaining the price down to much lower than the original quote. "I live here. You can't charge me that" said in an emphatic, no-nonsense voice, usually works and the fare drops. The cheapest flight she could find for one of her trips to Ghana was a much longer route via Dubai. "Sure it was a long journey but they gave me the lowest price—and I had never seen Dubai!"

When her children were small, she often bought their clothes in Accra's second-hand clothing market, a maze of narrow streets and laneways overflowing with mounds of shoes, blue jeans, bras and T-shirts, all at rock-bottom prices. "When I am in Ghana, I always marvel at how easy it is to live with less," she says. "The Ghanaians I know can live without all the modern energy-guzzling amenities equated with progress. They can manage on so little. Why can't we?"

She also shuns any suggestion that she purchase a 4-wheel drive van to provide transport for herself and the libraries. She claims that it would only signal that OCLF is a rich NGO from overseas and that would give the wrong image to those she serves. Until recently, she relied on a 1986 Nissan taxi, typical of most of the cabs in Accra. Then, in 2008, she met Kwame Katsekpor, a gentle man with an infectious laugh and a warm smile. He, too, drove an unreliable vehicle so Kathy struck a deal with him: she would buy him a newer vehicle (he chose a 1998 Nissan Primera) and he would pay Kathy back in small instalments. In return, he would offer her free transportation during her visits, providing she paid for the petrol. In a few years, he will own the car. Kwame was delighted with what he called a 'win-win' situation and promptly attached a Canadian flag to his dashboard.

Joanna's gentle knock on the door well before 7 a.m. signals the start of another day for Kathy. She dons a simple shift of African cotton or a skirt featuring the words 'Joy of Reading' across the fabric, slips into a pair of sandals and lathers on sunscreen. While she is enjoying breakfast, there comes the first knock on the door. It could be the plumber asking for money to repair a leaking pipe. It could be the electrician regarding some ceiling fans that need to be replaced. It could be the carpenter needing funds to purchase materials for furniture. It could be the tiler who has, not for the first time, miscalculated his needs and requires more money to purchase more tiles.

Between the visits from tradesmen, there are others: the baker's granddaughter has just arrived with two loaves of crocodile bread—a loaf of bread shaped like a crocodile—for a library party, and a young girl passes by to collect money for her class exams. Once, on the day before the library opening in Goi, an urgent call came from the workmen asking if they should buy "one goat or two?"

More often than not, the early morning visitor could be a staff member begging for a loan to help pay for their rent (rents in Ghana must be paid three years in advance) or for a family funeral (a huge burden for most) or for a hospital visit. Kathy finds these requests the toughest to handle, partly because she has a generous heart and finds it hard to say 'no' but also, she has learned from experience that loans are hard to keep track of and are seldom paid back.

She is now trying another approach which has so far worked well. When Ayisha, a teenage library member, asked for money for prescription glasses which her family could not afford, Kathy agreed but only after putting her to work helping for several hours at an evening function. On another occasion, Rosemary, a member of the drama troupe, requested a large loan to complete a business course. Her father had promised to see her through the course but had abandoned the family and his commitment to his daughter. Before Kathy agreed to the request, she devised a way for Rosemary to earn the money. The girl was a gifted seamstress so Kathy asked her to sew 100 bags for OCLF's Library-in-a-Bag project. She also asked Rosemary to turn up at the Nima Library for three hours every morning during the school summer vacation and give special coaching to four children who were poor readers. It worked well for both sides. "The demands never seem to stop," sighs Kathy. "I spend much of my time dealing with these types of requests."

Occasionally, a child who wants nothing more than a little TLC (tender loving care) will also turn up unannounced in the early hours. One Saturday morning, three young girls, all about 11 years old, arrived at 7 a.m. "We want to greet you," they said to a surprised Kathy who was still gulping down her breakfast. She dropped everything, moved to the outside veranda and read them the story of *Jeremiah Learns to Read*. She then gave each child a paper and pencil and asked them to write a letter to the book's author. They started at once. Within minutes, they handed over their letters. "Thank you, Madam Katty," one of them said. "Now I can teach my mother to read. She loves to sing but she can't say any of the letters." Kathy snapped a photo of all three before they skipped happily away.

Most mornings begin with the arrival of driver Kwame ready to start the day. He usually arrives just before 8 a.m.—and nearly always on time— and Kathy's day of non-stop errands begins: a visit to the A.M.A. to push them yet again on the salary issue; a stop at the bank to check on the arrival, or not, of transferred funds; another stop at two different sites in opposite ends of the city to see if they are suitable for a new library; a visit to one or more of the libraries to help iron out staff issues and offer encouragement and support. Once, it was a stop at a prison where a former library member had been locked up for being caught with a gun in his bag. Could Kathy try and help arrange his release? She never stops for a sit-down lunch but picks up her favourite fried yam with fresh pepper sauce or roasted plantain from the roadside and eats it on the move. The long journeys through the dense Accra traffic are the perfect time to catch up on phone calls and handle dozens of outstanding details that require attention. Now that she has email access on her new cell phone, she can accomplish twice as much on those long road trips.

It is not surprising that, in recent visits, Kathy admits to feeling "so-o-o tired" by the end of the day. Her project is expanding and, with each passing year, the demands—and the frustrations—mount. Her newest and largest library is a tall two-story structure built on the grounds of the Accra College of Education in the north end of Accra and bordering Madina, a large impoverished area. Unlike her other libraries, this one was partnered with the Ghana Education Service (GES) which agreed much earlier to pay staff salaries and utilities.

The building was completed and ready to open in May 2011. However, there was a serious glitch. Since the building faced a busy road with constant traffic, Kathy insisted that it would not open until the city provided a traffic light to allow the children to cross safely, something that was stipulated in the original agreement. She remembered all too clearly that during the sod-turning ceremony for the Nima Centre, a small child was killed trying to cross the busy road. The last thing she wanted was to have this happen again.

A simple request? Not so. A full year before the completion of the building, she began making phone calls and writing letters and emails to the appropriate authorities asking them to install a traffic light at the crossing. She visited the Ministry of Transport office, the A.M.A.—anyone who could help grant the required permission. Everyone was sympathetic to the idea but no one made it happen.

She then changed her approach. If a traffic light wasn't possible, could they install speed bumps to slow down the speeding cars? Well... Not sure...We'll see... More time passed with no action.

Kathy had planned an opening in May 2011 while she was in Ghana. But, to her disappointment, the launch date arrived and there were still no speed bumps. Reluctantly, she decided to leave the completed building closed and returned to Canada. She hated to see the building sitting empty when so many children were waiting to enjoy it, but she knew if she opened it, the safety issue would never be resolved. Given that staff members had been assigned and were ready to work, she arranged for them to visit nearby schools to initiate library programs and thus keep the momentum going and the children happy.

She continued to press the issue from Canada calling everyone she knew who might help. Week after week, reports would trickle in that 'Yes, yes. We're working on it.' Even a scathing article by Salifu Abdul-Rahaman in the *Ghanaian Times*, carrying a bold headline that read "$500,000 Library Abandoned" made little difference.

Kathy returned to Ghana six months later in early November 2011. The very day she landed, two men turned up and dug the first holes for the speed bumps. It took another two weeks to finish the job which allowed her time to prepare a hastily organized commissioning of the new library. Miraculously, with even more urging, there is now a full-time crossing guard to help the children cross the road safely.

Kathy has learned from long experience that what is crucial for working in the developing world is patience. "If you're not a patient person, it would be impossible to move forward because there are so many obstacles and decisions take forever and a day." She has acquired a fair amount of patience since the start of her library project, but with the never-ending hurdles she faces, she still needs it in abundance. "Not many people realize just how difficult it is to work here," she sighs after one particularly challenging day. "On top of what we do here, there is also the arduous task of fundraising here and in Canada which takes so much time and energy. Few Ghanaians involved in our project have any idea how hard it is to raise money to build these facilities."

The commissioning of the new library later that month brought together 50 staff members from the OCLF libraries, teachers and pupils from the local schools and a sizable contingent of government officials. The senior students covered the building with balloons and ribbons and draped coloured cloths from the blue tiled mosaic pillars. The college choir and dancers from a nearby school both gave lively performances.

Then Kathy rose and stood at the microphone to welcome the guests. She paid tribute to those who had played a part in creating the building— Roger Amenyogbe, the architect, project manager Kojo Maclean and all her loyal workmen. Then she turned to face the row of government officials, extended her thanks, somewhat ironically, for finally enabling her to open the new library. Then, drawing on the confidence she has developed over the years, she reminded them that the library was still short three staff members!

THE ONE CONSTANT THAT HELPS GROUND KATHY AND ENABLES HER TO tackle the many challenges that turn up is her home away from home in Nima. At the end of each long day, when the intense brightness of the sunlight is on the wane, she picks up her camera and strolls through the neighbourhood to practise her favourite pastime: taking pictures, most often for the photo-illustrated books she started publishing a few years earlier. This day, she is looking for striped objects for a book of stripes to add to the seven books of colours she has already produced and is delighted to have found a child holding a striped bag and another with a multi-coloured striped shirt. She leads them to a suitable backdrop and clicks dozens of shots. Once she is satisfied with the photos, she seeks out the childrens' parents to ask their permission to use them in her next book.

She then returns home to the guesthouse just as the tropical sun transforms the sky above Nima into a splash of brilliant orange and hundreds of fruit bats swarm to their evening resting place. This is the time when the whole community comes alive with animated chatter and throbbing music and the street sellers are setting up wooden tables piled high with pyramids of bananas and avocado pears and grapefruit-size mangoes. A woman is cooking doughnuts in sizzling oil or preparing *kelewele,* fried plantain seasoned with a liberal dash of ginger and hot pepper. Further along, a young girl sits patiently while her aunty weaves the strands of her black hair into dozens of intricate braids. The smell of spicy food permeates the air.

Many of the sellers wave a friendly greeting to Kathy as she passes. She takes the time to speak to them all, asking one about a family member, another about a sick relative or a new baby. The children all rush to encircle her. One evening, unable to extricate herself from the crowd around her, she plucked a book from her knapsack, sat down on the front steps of the guesthouse, gathered all the children around and read them a story. She called it "my library on the steps."

Then she enters into the relative quiet of the guesthouse, greets Joanna and Jennifer, and collapses into a chair. After dinner, she stretches out on her bed, props her computer on her lap, checks her emails and reviews the photos she has taken that day. The only thing that prevents her from working long into the night is the occasional onset of migraines or infrequent muscle spasms in her back and legs.

Some people question the wisdom and safety of living in Nima where unsavoury elements exist, but Kathy has never doubted the choice. "I love living so close to the people we serve," she says. "I feel such a close kinship with all of them. I know many of the children and their parents and grandparents. No matter where they meet, Ghanaians greet each other with a warmth and concern that is very touching. They show a great respect for their elders and a genuine kindness not only to each other, but especially to strangers.

"Indeed, I count myself so lucky to be part of this community."

## CHAPTER 15

# OCLF's Valued Volunteers

VOLUNTEERS HAVE ALWAYS BEEN A VITALLY IMPORTANT PART OF KATHY'S project, both in Ghana and in Canada. When word about the libraries in Ghana began to spread beyond her own circle of friends and family, bags and boxes of books would arrive daily on her doorstep in Winnipeg. As the piles mounted, she soon realized she needed help to sort and pack them.

It was about this time that Winnipeg resident Joan Graham read in the local paper that Kathy was looking for books to send to Ghana so she carried over an armful. Joan already had a strong but sad connection with Ghana: her only son Paul, then just 21, had been working there as a geologist with a mining company and was tragically killed in a car crash. "When I first arrived at Kathy's," she recalled,"I remember saying to her 'If you ever need any help...' That was in 1997. I have been here ever since."

The first day Joan arrived at Kathy's home, she remembers being ushered into the dining room where the table was covered with beach towels to protect the surface. "I sat down with Kathy and we started covering books with plastic, then packed them into boxes. We packed about 50 boxes that year, then about 60 the next year." Kathy showed no shame in asking any travellers to Ghana to carry over a box or two.

Since then, as the needs continued to grow, more volunteers joined Joan around Kathy's dining table providing important support to her ever-expanding project. Sally Irwin, a former nurse and one of Kathy's longest-standing Winnipeg friends, does "anything that needs to be done," from covering books to embroidering hand towels for the libraries with the word 'READ' and a happy face. Alice Moulton, a former teacher who once heard Kathy speak and was "so blown away I just had to help" puts her delicate handwriting skills to work to acknowledge by hand many of the donations from supporters.

Kathy Parry, who once lived with her husband in northern Ghana, has turned out to be an expert at packing books, a massive job especially when preparing a whole container of books for shipment to Ghana. "We check every single book that comes in," she explains as she neatly packs a stack of newly cleaned-up books into a carton. Books that aren't culturally appropriate, or are even slightly damaged, are sent elsewhere. Where necessary, the volunteers clean up pencil marks, fingerprints and erase names. Then they wipe them clean, staple the spines to reinforce soft-cover books and stamp each one with the OCLF name before packing them into cartons lined with plastic—in case they end up sitting on a dockside in the rain.

Finally, they tape the box shut and label it—primary, secondary, reference—with the number and type of books in each box. They also note the weight of each box—a weigh scale sits squarely in the front hall for that purpose. They then place all the boxes at one end of the dining room waiting for Kathy's husband John to lug them downstairs to the basement.

Over the years, John has done more than his share of lifting boxes. As he stands glancing around the dining room which often looks more like a publisher's warehouse than the family's dining room, he points to one end of the crowded room. "This end is the incoming side," he says, as he hauls in another box of books which has been dropped off on the doorstep. "The other end is the outgoing side, waiting for me to carry them downstairs. It works quite well until we have the whole family here and need to clear the table for dinner!"

All the packed books are stored in the basement where the boxes are sandwiched between numerous bikes and skis, hockey sticks and paint cans to await shipment to Ghana. Since the once-generous airlines are no longer able to ship boxes for free, Kathy must rely on willing travellers or wait until there are enough boxes to fill a container. In 2006, she sent their first container filled with 80,000 books. Another went off in 2011. This will be the last big shipment of books from Canada since culturally appropriate children's books are now more available in Ghana. Luckily, there are still travellers from Canada who are willing to carry one or two boxes of books and libraries supplies with them to Ghana.

"There is always so much going on here," says Joan in a classic understatement. Besides dealing with the books, the volunteers help keep track of all the contributions, send out the annual appeal letters, help acknowledge donations, pack up two huge 50 pound boxes for each of Kathy's twice-yearly trips to Ghana. "It's a busy place," says Joan. "But then, Kathy thrives on a lot of stuff going on at the same time. I've rarely seen her tired, or annoyed. And her patience is amazing. Why, she's even patient with telemarketers!"

The busiest time in the Knowles' house is every September when the volunteers work flat out to send around 500 annual appeal letters to interested family and friends and previous donors. Then they are on full alert when replies and donations begin to arrive. In 2012, they received donations totalling just over $350,000. These come from people of all ages and from all walks of life, from people who have never been to Africa and who couldn't find Ghana on a map. "But still, they open their hearts and give," says Kathy in wide-eyed amazement. The volunteers answer every contribution with a handwritten note attached to one of Kathy's recent photos from Ghana and a thank-you letter from one of the library members. "It is a huge amount of work but it is the least we can do for those who are generous enough to help us."

THE VOLUNTEERS ALSO PRINT AND ADDRESS INVITATIONS FOR ALL Kathy's speaking presentations. Over the years, she has given talks in schools and churches and libraries in various cities across Canada, as well as appearances in North Carolina and California. Early on, she felt nervous and uncomfortable standing before an audience of anywhere from 25 to more than 100 people. But with many such presentations behind her, she has become more accustomed to the spotlight.

Audiences always react to her talks with enthusiasm. They are impressed by her words, by her sincerity and by her obvious passion for what she is doing. "So inspiring" is what you hear among the post-presentation chatter. People line up afterwards, pressing her with questions. How can we help? Where can we send a donation? She enjoys talking about her project and meeting supporters across the country. She also recognizes that these presentations are an important means of spreading the word and of garnering funds for her next library.

Her talks have occasionally turned up unexpected surprises. In a presentation she gave at the National Library and Archives in Ottawa in 2005, she included among her photos one of Rudolph, a tall lanky librarian, who was obliged to walk several kilometres each day to his library job. After her speech, a man in the audience approached Kathy, thanked her for her presentation and handed her an envelope. Inside she found a $100 bill. "This is to buy a bicycle for Rudolph," he explained. She tucked the money away and on her next visit to Ghana, purchased the bike for a delighted Rudolph.

While the volunteers pack or sort books or acknowledge donations, Kathy moves from the frenzied activity in the dining room, through the large living room with a grand piano in one end and her viola propped up in a corner. She steps into the adjoining kitchen and heats up a pot of soup for her volunteers. She never stops singing their praises. "It is our volunteers who are the strength of our organization," she says. "Indeed, they are the most loyal group you could find, turning up without fail two, sometimes three days a week, year after year." It is because of their help—and the fact that Kathy takes no salary herself and is meticulous about every penny she spends—that the organization has managed to keep its administration and fundraising costs to an impressive one to two percent, far lower than most NGOs whose costs for administration often reach anywhere from ten to 20 percent.

It is also because Kathy is renowned for her frugality. "Every penny we save means there is more for the children," she reminds everyone constantly. The volunteers are encouraged to re-use envelopes, to cut note cards from large sheets of card stock and to canvas friends (and cultivate the local liquor store) for all their boxes and packing materials. Kathy also shuns personal luggage on her travels to Ghana so she can carry the maximum amount of books and supplies.

On all her overseas flights, she routinely asks the airlines (and encourages others to do so) for their used first-class face cloths which would otherwise be thrown away. With a good wash by Joanna, they are ready to hand over to library staff to wipe down dusty books and shelves. KLM flight attendants have now become familiar with the request. "For the libraries in Ghana?" they ask."Certainly."

AS THE ORGANIZATION GREW, KATHY DECIDED TO SHIFT HER 'OFFICE' out of her bedroom to a room on the third floor. There are now two desks, one for her which is cluttered with papers and pens and pictures of her children, another for the volunteers. The wall is covered with photos of smiling Ghanaian children, kids' letters and poems. Bookshelves bulge with papers, a collection of filing cabinets is bursting at the seams and mementos from dozens of visits are scattered hither and yon. The phone rings constantly with its cheerful sing-song bell which provides background music in what Kathy calls "our organized chaos." While she is in Canada, she often works until 11.45 p.m. and occasionally wakes up at 3 a.m. to reach government offices in Ghana.

There are constant demands on her time and generosity. She seizes any chance to support a local charity. If a friend tells her about a raffle, she'll buy a ticket. If a silent auction isn't doing well, she'll sign her name for everything. She still tries to meet the two friends to practise their string trio every week. "I need that commitment or I would never see my friends."

Thanks to Kathy's army of dedicated volunteers, the Osu Children's Library Fund functions with no paid staff in Canada. Also, Kathy takes no salary herself. She is often asked if she has ever considered hiring staff in order to ease her load. "No, I just couldn't do it," she replies emphatically. "Fortunately, there have always been people who are willing to help. I am blessed to have such a loyal team of volunteers who have been such a great support. If I were to hire myself, for example, how would I put a dollar figure on what I do? I just couldn't do it. And it wouldn't be fair to our staff in Ghana because I know how hard they work for such modest pay. Luckily for me, John's salary is enough to put a roof over our head."

IN THE TWO DECADES SINCE IT BEGAN, THE ANNUAL BUDGET OF the OCLF has crept up from zero to around $350,000, raised largely by small donations from hundreds of Canadians. Kathy struggles to keep all the grant proposals and reports up-to-date and is only too happy to rely on Bonnie Gailfus, an accountant based in Calgary, who handles the books and keeps track of all donations coming in as well as the funds being transferred to Ghana. "Thank heavens for Bonnie," says Kathy. "She is aware of all the libraries we support and keeps detailed records of funds we receive and those we spend. It is Bonnie who submits our annual report to Revenue Canada and to our auditors. With Bonnie on side, I am completely confident that all the finances are in good hands."

Financial records are audited annually and Beth Lennard uses her extensive business experience to help oversee the finances. She also acts as chairman of the five-person board of directors who helped prepare the following Mission Statement outlining the aims of the OCLF:

> *To develop a network of libraries designed to promote reading for children and literacy opportunities for adults who have not attended school;*
>
> *To extend the outreach services of each library where there is community and financial support;*
>
> *To seek and encourage the involvement of local communities, to respect their ideas and contributions and to help them to strive towards sustainability in their projects;*
>
> *To maintain close working relationships with local authorities whose financial support is vital to the long-term sustainability of the libraries.*

OVER THE LAST 15 YEARS, WHILE VOLUNTEERS HAVE CONTINUED TO help out on the home front, another type of volunteer has emerged in the form of many young and not-so-young volunteers who are flying to Ghana to help out in the libraries there. These are people of every age and background who bring their skills—and enthusiasm—to work with library staff. They not only provide practical help but, more importantly, they often forge deep friendships with Ghanaians, making it a mutually enriching experience.

Not all of those who apply are suitable and an extensive screening is part of the process to ensure that the candidate will fit in with the project. Over the years, OCLF has welcomed more than two dozen full-time volunteers in Ghana. Only one, a young man in his early 20s who was the first of five CIDA interns, didn't fit and he returned early to Canada.

The number of volunteers is kept intentionally low since accommodation is tight and, being a relatively small project, placements are limited. Some come for a few weeks, others for three to six months. Many seem to have caught the OCLF bug. Take Penny Giaccone, a primary school teacher from Ottawa, and her daughter Callie. They spent part of the summer of 2011 as volunteers in Ghana. Penny returned the following year with Callie and her elder sister, Sophia, and is already planning another visit. Almost without exception, volunteers have declared that their experience in Ghana was a transformative one.

Volunteers often work on their own and are expected to bring new ideas to challenge and engage the children and the adult learners. The most important requirement is that they enjoy children. Those with teaching experience, especially at the lower grades, or working at summer camps or community centres benefit most. Schools in Ghana rarely include any type of creative activities, so volunteers with an interest in teaching educational games and introducing arts and crafts or music have the most to offer.

OCLF follows the example of most other NGOs in asking volunteers to cover the cost of their transport to Ghana, all vaccinations, malaria tablets, health and evacuation insurance and their in-country living expenses. They are also expected to raise or donate $2,000 to OCLF. This is not an administrative fee but helps support OCLF's outreach and, more importantly, helps to demonstrate a commitment to the project. Volunteers have found imaginative ways to raise the required funds: some have organized a used-book sale, or a concert. Others have sent letters to family members and friends seeking their support. One volunteer made and sold hundreds of perogies to those in her community.

OCLF has found that its volunteers can often become excellent ambassadors for the organization when they return home. Some have written articles in their local newspaper to spread the word about the organization. Others have become donors or have shared stories with their friends and families who then become donors.

Of all the volunteers who have helped out in Ghana, a few stand out. One is Rosanna Nicol from Ottawa who, then 19, spent five months with OCLF in early 2007. Rosanna had finished her first year at the University of King's College in Halifax, had already travelled widely, but had never been to Africa.

She stayed at the guesthouse in Nima and was placed at the Mamprobi Library. This meant starting each day with a 20 minute walk to catch a tro-tro for an hour and a half journey to the library. "This commute was rich with interesting encounters," she told me later. "I had many a chat about religion, poverty, development, gender roles, whether I was married and if not, was I interested? All this while we were moving slowly through congested traffic."

Rosanna worked closely with the two librarians and helped them work out a daily schedule. Each morning, they would organize the books, sign in the children as they began to arrive, teach them new games—Boggle and Bingo were the most popular—or act out scenes from storybooks. A special treat was a 'poetry slam' she helped organize at two of the libraries and encouraged library members to write and share their own poems. And every afternoon, she would gather the children together on an outdoor bench for the ever-popular story time. She also brought along her guitar and taught them some of her favourite campfire songs.

Rosanna's most lasting contribution was, together with her friend and fellow volunteer, Suzanna Showler, to gather a group of girls from Nima and the neighbouring Maamobi to form a girls football (soccer) team. Every Saturday morning at 5 a.m. during their five-month placement, they met with the girls for weekly practices. This was a first for women in the area, especially for the Muslim girls who would even turn up for matches during Ramadan, the holy month of fasting, when they would be obliged to play on empty stomachs. Before the two left Ghana, they found a young Ghanaian man, Ambrose Nazzah, to take over the team which became known as the Nimobi Ladies Football Club which today competes in city-wide matches.

Rosanna returned to Canada, completed her university degree and had the distinction of winning a Rhodes Scholarship to study at Oxford University. She has no doubt that her experience in Ghana strengthened her application and played a part in her acceptance of this prestigious award.

ANOTHER VOLUNTEER, EMILIE WALL, A FORMER PRIMARY SCHOOL teacher and grandmother of two from Portage la Prairie in Manitoba, arrived in Ghana in 2006. She spent most of her month-long placement at the library in Goi, the small fishing village east of Accra. Following her stay, she jotted down some of the highlights of her days: waking to the sounds of roosters crowing; recognizing how precious water is in Africa and how quickly you can adapt to bathing with very little; hearing the nursery school children waiting to enter the library, chanting "We want to learn, we want to learn;" discovering the children's love of music and their excitement when she taught them new rhymes, finger plays and songs; hearing the cry of fear when a small child first saw 'the white lady;' attending the funeral of a ten-year-old boy; watching the fishermen bring in their catch of the day; working in the library and seeing the children enjoy the books and develop a love of reading. "But above all," wrote Emilie "I will always remember how the people of Goi taught me much about the richness of life lived simply and graciously. My volunteer time was an experience of a lifetime."

WINNIPEG STUDENT MARINA GOODWIN WAS LOOKING FOR SOMEWHERE to undertake a volunteer placement for the practical component of her International Development degree at the University of Winnipeg when a friend put her in touch with Kathy. In early 2010, she left snowy Winnipeg and 24 hours later landed in Accra to begin her four-month placement.

She spent two months in the Osu Library helping Joanna with activities for the children. They drew pictures, made friendship bracelets, sang songs, and held an afternoon of track-and-field games as a tribute to the Winter Olympics in Canada. "It was a little tough trying to make the Winter Olympics relevant to 30 children who had never seen snow but they loved it."

For the second half of her placement, Marina travelled to Ho, the district capitol of the Volta Region, to help in a small library that was housed in a classroom of St. Cecilia's Parish School. She lived with Mawunyo Klu, the librarian, and together they organized reading timetables for the students and worked out different activities. She showed them how to make beads from rolled-up paper. She read stories to the pupils and taught them songs. One afternoon, she visited the nursery side of the school and taught about 90 kindergarten students (many of whom couldn't understand English) the words of *Hokey Pokey*. "It was hilarious."

Marina admits that, when she first arrived in Ghana, she was overwhelmed by the onslaught of all the sights, smells and sounds. By the time she left, she felt as though she was leaving a family behind. "Volunteering with the OCLF in Ghana has been one of the most amazing and altering experiences of my life. It both defined and surpassed all my expectations and I hope someday I can return."

WHEN AMERICAN JOURNALIST THERESA MORROW LEARNED THAT HER husband had received a Fulbright grant to teach for a year at the University of Ghana, she asked if there was some way she could help in the libraries. Kathy had long since felt that most of the older library members could benefit from a writing program in which they would learn the elements of creative writing and creative thinking, skills that are not taught in Ghana's school system. She put the idea to Theresa who was up to the challenge: she combed through books, attended workshops and contacted educators and literacy specialists to help her devise a program that would suit the children.

Within weeks of arriving in Ghana, Theresa had organized two groups of children, one in Osu Library and the other in the new Madina Library. Anywhere from ten to 15 eager children met twice a week around a table, pen and paper in hand. Most of them had little experience writing anything beyond their own name and a few school exercises and they were shy and uncertain at first. According to Theresa, "once they got the idea, they were off and running."

Theresa talked first about the different elements that make up a story: the character, the setting, the problem to overcome and finally the solution. She helped them write stories about animals, about themselves, about their families. They also wrote about their dreams. One boy chose a goat as his character. On the way to school, the boy noticed that the tro-tro driver was not a human at all but a goat dressed in human clothes. When the tro-tro ran out of fuel, the driver called on his friend Brother Super Goat to help out. Super Goat arrived and flew the whole tro-tro to the petrol station.

Another child, also describing one of her dreams, wrote about finding a leopard under her bed. She named the animal 'Under-the-Bed' and one day, took him to a football match between Ghana and Germany. It turned out that Ghana was losing the game, so 'Under-the-Bed' leapt onto the field and scored the winning goal!

As part of a description exercise, one girl wrote that her house "is as wide as a lion's mouth." Another, writing about "My Earliest Memory," described his feelings when his father got his first job. "When my father had a job, it was the best day in my family because it was the first time my father had a job."

One thing Theresa realized was that girls had a harder time than boys getting outside their immediate experience. They tended to copy familiar ideas rather than come up with their own. They also did not turn up as regularly as the boys since many of them had to return home after school to help with family chores. "The girls need a lot of extra encouragement to think creatively and with confidence," Theresa pointed out. "Many of them do not know how to dream."

Nonetheless, Theresa found it a great experience watching the development of her students. In no time, they began to enjoy "painting pictures with words." This opened up a whole new world to children who normally are only taught to learn by rote. The proof was that they came week after week after a full day of school. They sat down with a pencil and paper and, after settling in for a few minutes, they put their heads down and wrote. One group proudly called themselves the Talented Writing Club, the other the Imagination Famous Writing Club.

For Theresa, the rewards were many. "Watching those little minds being set free, seeing that split second when they realized they could write anything they wanted and no one would judge them. I saw it happen over and over. They went into that writing trance and pulled the most amazing stories out of their minds."

IN JULY 2010, A CANADIAN FAMILY ARRIVED FOR A MONTH TO HELP out as volunteers. Gillian Williamson is a kindergarten teacher in Ottawa and her three children, Sara, then 22, Julia, 20 and Alex, 18, were all seeking a developing world experience. They arranged a home exchange with an expatriate family returning to Ottawa for the summer, so they had the added challenge of daily market shopping and cooking their own meals.

They divided the family in two. Gillian and Alex worked at the Nungua Library while Sara and Julia helped out at the Osu Library. Halfway through the month, they switched. Every evening, they met back at home and shared their adventures. They would then work out lesson plans and schedules of crafts, songs, and games for the next day.

It was a month of rich experiences: learning to play *ampe*, a fast-paced game of jumping and clapping; teaching a youth of 19 who had never gone to school or learned to read and cheering him on when he finally managed to read c-a-t. They helped an elderly fisherman struggling to learn to read in English and they were amazed to meet children who, even as they wander dusty paths in their bare feet, dream of continuing their education and becoming teachers or doctors. It was especially rich for Alex. He arrived in Ghana shy and overwhelmed but finally managed to experience the satisfaction of teaching others how to play the guitar or the keyboard or drums. It was Alex who turned out to be the saddest to leave.

On her return home, Sara Williamson, a graduate of Mount Allison University in Sackville, New Brunswick, wrote a wrap-up piece about the family's stay in Ghana. "Kathy Knowles, you have started something truly incredible," she wrote. "In and outside of the walls of the OCLF libraries, entire communities of people are coming together to share their talents and their knowledge. Over by the windows, a voice sounds out its first word read off a page, while outside, a chorus of voices rises in song. Fingers work busily to create beautiful things, and students smile proudly over their work.

"A young playwright watches a group of teenagers rehearsing his work, in roles that examine their culture and speak of our common humanity. Here at the tables, students sit reading from shelves and shelves of books. Day after day they are drawn here after school simply because this is genuinely exciting for them, and they're happy to have the opportunity.

"It's an honour to have been part of such a phenomenal project, and it goes without saying that our worlds are changed by the experience. So many worlds are changed by the libraries—these bright, beautiful spaces bustling with activity, creativity, connection, learning and laughter.

"More than anything," she wrote, "we'll remember the laughter."

## CHAPTER 16

# Reaching out to the Disabled

WHEN MICHAËLLE JEAN VISITED THE NIMA LIBRARY, ONE OF THE CHIL-
dren who sat listening to her read a story was Masawoud Zakari, then
a boy of ten who was carried into the building by a library member, his
spindly legs permanently bent and tucked under his bottom. In most
countries of the world, he would hardly be noticed. But in Ghana, his
presence in the Nima Library represented one of Kathy's most important victories.

Kathy's preoccupation with books and literacy is easily matched
by her special concern for children with disabilities. Whenever she is
in Ghana, she is always looking out for any chance to help. In western
countries, most of those with disabilities have access to special medical
help, a chance to attend school, to find a job. They live in a society that
increasingly respects their needs. But in Ghana, youngsters with disabilities or deformities—no matter how minor—often face a lifetime of
rejection and their lot is either to work the streets begging for handouts
or to stay at home, hidden from society.

In fact, when UNICEF tried to survey the number of African children with disabilities, they were frustrated to find that most of them
were nowhere to be seen, hidden away and out of sight. Many believe
they carry evil spirits, frighten people or bring shame on the family.
They are teased at school, harassed in their communities and would
rarely be hired for a job. In short, they are considered to be a blight on
society and receive the most meagre help, if any, from the government
or their communities.

Kathy had already shown her concern for those with disabilities by inviting a teacher of sign language to the Nima Library to introduce it to library members. "It's about creating awareness," she says. "Most children in Ghana rarely see handicapped kids so they don't think about their needs or frustrations."

Kathy's first opportunity to help address this injustice came in 1996 when she visited the School for the Blind in the hilltop village of Akropong, the largest facility for blind children in Ghana. She had earlier purchased two tactile/Braille books in Canada and, on her next visit to Ghana, she passed by the school to deliver the books and to see what library facilities they had.

The village of Akropong is a one-hour drive northeast of Accra on a strikingly beautiful road that snakes up through the wooded hills. A sharp turn off the main road leads into the school compound, a collection of time-worn buildings. The school houses 275 students, most of them victims of river blindness, a disease which is transmitted to humans through an infected black fly bite. It is the major cause of blindness in several parts of the continent, including West Africa, although recent international efforts have made some headway towards eradicating the disease.

On that first visit to the school, Kathy met Nancy Kutornu, a Grade 2 teacher. She took Kathy to see the school's library—a dark and dusty room filled with decades-old magazines and a few musty Braille textbooks. There were no materials for young readers and not a single storybook in Braille.

Kathy spread the word in Canada asking for books and educational materials for visually-impaired children. Several organizations in Canada and the US rallied with educational games and children's storybooks overprinted with Braille. On her next trip to Ghana, she carried over a 70 pound box of materials for blind and partially-sighted children.

They were delighted to receive the materials but there was nowhere safe to store them so Nancy had to keep them in her apartment on the school's grounds. Kathy told the school principal that, if he would designate one of the classrooms as a library, she would furnish it with tables, chairs and shelves and provide more books and games. They agreed to release an unused classroom and named Nancy as the librarian. She immediately signed up for library training with Joanna.

Local volunteers helped empty the room, scrub the floor, install louvered windows and ceiling fans. Kathy arranged for her painter to brighten up the room and commissioned her carpenter to make suitable furniture. They then placed a washstand with a basin, towel and soap at the front door.

On her next trip to Ghana, Kathy visited Akropong for the official opening. When she arrived, dozens of children were waiting patiently for their first experience of a real library. After the ribbon-cutting, the first group of children dutifully washed their hands and stepped inside. Each one walked slowly and cautiously across the room, their fingers dancing across the open shelves feeling the Braille books. For all these pupils, this was their first introduction to storybooks.

It was a small start but one that would have a lasting effect on the students in that school.

NANCY KUTORNU SPENT MANY LONG HOURS ENSURING THAT THE NEW facility functioned well. She was not only the school librarian, she was also the mother of Emmanuel, then aged ten. Emmanuel was a bright and curious boy who had been born severely handicapped by cerebral palsy. His mind was alert, but his speech was awkward and his legs were too weak to support his weight. Nancy had not been able to find a school that would accept him so he spent his days alone in their one-room apartment dragging himself across the floor.

Kathy was concerned that a lad as bright as Emmanuel was not in school so she and Nancy made several inquiries, pleading with teachers and headmasters to accept him. After a long search, Nancy found a school that would take her son. He could start the following year in class 1—well behind his age group. But it was a start. Since then, he has progressed well.

Emmanuel had just started school when Kathy came up with another of her brainwaves. Since the boy had seldom ventured outside his mother's apartment and since the children in her libraries had rarely, if ever, met a handicapped child, she decided to hire a taxi that would accommodate Emmanuel's wheelchair and transport him and his mother down to Accra to the Mamprobi Library. The next week, a beaming Emmanuel arrived with Nancy at the library where more than 100 children sat patiently on floor mats waiting for the visitors.

Kathy introduced the two guests, explaining to the children why she had invited the pair to the library. Nancy spoke first. She explained, in her soft, gentle voice, how Emmanuel had come to be born handicapped, what he could and could not do, the frustrations and the problems she faced in bringing up such a child. "During Emmanuel's birth, they had to use forceps and because his head was soft, his brain was damaged. I knew from that first day that something had happened to my baby. As he started to grow, I hoped each day that he would learn to stand up. But he never did." There was a hushed silence in the room.

Then it was Emmanuel's turn. He wheeled his chair forward and faced the children. He was clearly nervous and self-conscious but within minutes, he relaxed as he spoke about the difficulties he faced as a handicapped child. It was hard for him to write, he explained, but he was trying to learn to use a typewriter. "I must learn to write as I would like some day to be a doctor," he told them. As Emmanuel was nearing the end of his short talk, he looked out at the crowd of children and said, "Do you know what is the hardest part about being handicapped?" The children waited. "The hardest thing of all is to have no friends." He paused, thanked everyone for welcoming him then added with a broad grin, "This has been one of the happiest days of my life."

There was a split second of silence, then all the children jumped to their feet, clapping and cheering. One child after another rushed up to Emmanuel and stood beside him. "Emmanuel," said one, tugging at his sleeve "We all want to be your friend." They talked and laughed together, shared jokes and told stories. Some even exchanged addresses. Emmanuel could hardly contain his delight.

It came time to leave and the children gathered around the waiting taxi as Emmanuel was lifted in. The taxi moved slowly away as all the children waved goodbye. Emmanuel sat silently for a moment, then burst into tears. "The children spoke about that day for a long time," said Kathy. "I am sure most of them had never met a handicapped child before. Emmanuel taught them so much in that one afternoon."

A FEW YEARS AFTER EMMANUEL'S VISIT TO THE MAMPROBI LIBRARY, Kathy was sitting on the curved bench outside the Nima Centre after a long and tiring day when a young boy approached her, dragging himself along the pavement on his hands and knees. He looked no older than ten and he was bent double with his twisted feet tucked under his bottom. His upper body was fully formed, but his legs looked like spindly matchsticks and his knees and hands were covered with calluses.

He approached Kathy and introduced himself. "Hi. My name is Masawoud. Masawoud Zakari". And Kathy replied "And my name is Kathy. Where do you live?" "I live in Maamobi." And with barely a moment's a pause, he added "Would you like to see my home?"

A friend helped carry the lad across the Kanda Highway, and they proceeded to lead Kathy through a treacherous maze of Nima's laneways and into Maamobi, navigating the narrow pathways and open sewers with great skill. Finally, they entered the courtyard where the boy lived with his mother, Adama. The place was swarming with people. There were moms and grannies, a few dads, dozens of children and women preparing large pots of food over an open fire.

Adama, a woman of about 30, greeted Kathy. "*Akwaaba,*" she said as she pulled up a wobbly bench and signalled to Kathy to sit down. "This is where I live," said Masawoud in his shaky English.

It is unlikely that any foreigners had ever visited this tiny enclave so Kathy's presence was a big event. All eyes were on her as she struggled to speak a few words of *Twi* along with an improvised sign language. The atmosphere was warm and friendly as each person in turn stepped forward to greet her, shaking her hand and saying "*Akwaaba.*"

Kathy was moved by the reception. "I felt privileged to have been invited into this tiny community. Even though none of them spoke much English, they made me feel so welcome." She learned later that Masawoud's mother, Adama, was a fruit seller. "When I got to know her better, she came often to my guesthouse with an armful of fruit.

For someone who has so little herself, that was a precious gift." The following day, Kathy took Masawoud to the Nima Library and introduced him to the staff and some of the children and he quickly became a fixture in the place.

It didn't take Kathy long to learn Masawoud's sad story. He had been born in Kumasi, the largest city in central Ghana. His birth was a long and difficult one since his umbilical cord had wound itself tightly around his legs, pinning them under his bottom. He was also born with two club feet.

Masawoud's father took one look at his crippled son and vanished, leaving his mother to cope alone. If the family had had the money, a simple operation could have straightened out the boy's crooked legs and feet. But there was no money and, with a disabled child to care for, Adama was unable to work. She survived by snatching up other people's leftovers or by taking her baby onto the street and begging.

It was a tough and humiliating existence. Adama remembers friends saying to her "Why do you walk outside with that crippled boy? You should keep him hidden. Or at least hide his legs." It didn't help that Masawoud's grandmother told Adama that she should not waste money feeding and caring for the boy—especially since he would never be able to help his mother.

Most devastating of all was the day one of Adama's friends made a heartless suggestion. She told Adama it would be best if she were to poison her baby. "I said I couldn't possibly do that. I loved my baby too much." She never spoke to her 'friend' again.

Adama did her best to help her child. In 2001, she moved to Accra to be near her mother and her six siblings. Masawoud grew bigger but his legs remained like tiny sticks, still bent double. When he grew tired of 'walking' on his hands and knees, his mother or one of his friends had to carry him.

As he grew older, the pain increased. "People would constantly tease him," explained Adama, helped by a translator. "They would say he looked like an animal. The children in the library also teased him but he was so happy there, he didn't mind. He liked the library much more than his school."

Other children refused to eat with him, saying his hands must be full of dirt. Said Adama: "Every night, he would lie down and cry his heart out. 'They are laughing at me because I am crippled,' he would sob. He was also getting heavier to carry and no wheelchair could navigate the narrow laneways of Nima.

Soon after Kathy's first meeting with Masawoud, Arnaud Bouquet, a Canadian filmmaker, arrived in Ghana to make a film about Kathy and her work. Arnaud told her he wanted to feature two children whose lives had been changed by the presence of Kathy's libraries. One he chose was Masawoud.

When Arnaud first met Masawoud, he was struck by his beguiling smile. He was also impressed by the fighting spirit of the young boy who had suffered so much. He knew he would be a good subject for his film. The film was one episode in a series entitled "Partir pour ses Idées" ("Follow Your Dreams") and it was aired in French on Canadian television. Overnight, Masawoud became a star. "This relationship was a very important one," says Kathy. "Children respond well when someone cares about them. Suddenly, this boy was valued for who he is and that was very important."

Arnaud was so taken by Masawoud that he decided he wanted to help him. Before leaving Ghana, he learned that an orthopaedic surgeon from Britain paid regular visits to the Orthopedic Training Centre, a facility in the town of Nsawam, 40 kilometres northeast of Accra.

Arnaud arranged for the boy to be assessed and they agreed to accept him for surgery. They could start in five months' time but they warned Masawoud that it might require as many as six operations. The whole procedure would cost about $2,000 US.

Arnaud canvassed his family and friends and managed to raise the money. When the time came, Masawoud underwent the surgery. As predicted, he required six operations—two each on his hips, his knees and his feet—and braved the surgery like a true soldier. He was fitted with braces for his straightened legs and was given specially-made shoes and a pair of crutches. Six months after his first surgery, he returned home.

Kathy was in Ghana soon after Masawoud arrived home from the hospital. One day, she was standing at the gate of the Nima Library when suddenly the boy appeared in front of her. He was standing upright, supported by a pair of crutches and flashing a wide toothy grin. Then he took a few wobbly steps towards her and collapsed in her arms. "Look at me, Aunty Katty," he said beaming from ear to ear. "I'm walking."

Kathy was amazed. His was a journey with so much uncertainty. His mother had only a tiny income from selling fruit and there was hardly any outside support from the family or the community. His school had raised a little money so his mother could visit the hospital but that was all the help she received.

The transformation in the boy was remarkable. "For anyone to be confined to crawling and to suddenly have the freedom of mobility is amazing. It was not only the physical freedom he experienced. He was a person who had been virtually ignored. The operation elevated him into someone who was important." Masawoud was indeed born with the right name. It means, in *Hausa,* 'the lucky one.'

Adama too has taken on a new lease on life. Kathy urged her, as part of the deal, to attend literacy classes at the Nima Library. She attends sporadically and has made a start at learning English.

With his new mobility, Masawoud is now perpetually on the move. He darts along the precarious pathways of Maamobi like a mountain goat, up and down stairs, across the busy highway, along deeply-rutted laneways. One day, he said to Kathy "Did you know that I am a rap singer?" Without skipping a beat, Kathy asked him to write a song about the library. He and two friends whom he calls 'my back-up team,' sang their own song at a gathering at the Nima Centre with Masawoud cradling the microphone and swaying from side to side like a seasoned pop star. Kathy was so impressed that she arranged for the group, who called themselves "The Lucky Ones," to visit a small recording studio and the piece is now immortalized on a CD. Children in the community can still be heard clapping and singing the song *"One Saturday morning, I went to the library. I saw Kathy, teaching children…"*

No one is happier than Adama who still cannot believe the change in her son. "Every night when I pray, I say a big 'thank you' to all the friends who have made it possible for my son to stand on his own feet. They have given us so much to look forward to."

Kathy still marvels at the transformation of both Masawoud and his mother. "What is special about this boy is that he never blames others for his misfortunes, there is never a hint of 'why me?'" Even more commendable is the fact that he is constantly giving thanks to those who have helped him along the way.

Remarkable too is that fact that Masawoud, a keen soccer fan, has gathered together a group of his friends, formed his own football team and declared himself the coach. The name he has given his team is REPENT. They practice every afternoon—many of them in bare feet or plastic flip flops and on an uneven terrain—and are oblivious to the cows and sheep that wander across the field.

On one of Kathy's visits, she was about to leave for Canada when Masawoud told her he had something special to show her. "Let me escort you," he said leading the way down a back laneway. He pointed proudly to a cage sitting high on a ledge at the top of a house. "This is my dove," he said, beaming with pride. He explained that he had been given two cedis (about $1.50) at the mosque so he had decided to buy a dove. When Gibrine Adam, a friend of Kathy's and the distributor of a children's book about Masawoud called *The Lucky One*, he was amazed. "The boy could have bought anything with that money—chewing gum, food, a CD—and he chose to buy a dove. It is so beautiful!"

*The Lucky One*, the book OCLF published about Masawoud, features a full-face photo of the beaming boy on its cover. It has become one of the most popular books in the libraries and has been included in a biennial catalogue created by the International Board for Books for Young People (IBBY) which lists the best books from around the world that cater to children with disabilities. It also serves as a fitting tribute to a courageous young man.

## CHAPTER 17

# Spreading the Joy of Reading in Ghana—and Beyond

ALL THE TIME KATHY WAS OPENING LIBRARIES IN ACCRA, SHE WAS ALSO keeping a watchful eye on the many needs elsewhere in the country. The free training sessions run by Joanna brought a steady flow of teachers and would-be librarians seeking help and the skills to set up their own libraries. Each newly-trained person returned home with the model of Joanna's library firmly planted in their head and a carton of books tucked under their arm. Thanks largely to these training sessions, more than 200 facilities, large and small, have sprung up in most regions of Ghana.

Many of these began in a modest way before taking on a life of their own. One is St. Cecilia's Parish School in Ho, district capital of the Volta Region. Ho is a three-hour drive northeast of Accra on a road that crosses the Volta River and skirts the massive Akosombo Dam, the brainchild of Kwame Nkrumah who believed (falsely, it turned out) that the dam would provide enough electricity for the country.

Kathy learned that the school was keen to have a library, that they were willing to allocate a classroom for the purpose and that they would send Mawunyo Klu, one of their teachers, to Accra for training with Joanna. The school's support was unwavering and Mawunyo turned out to be a gifted and creative librarian. Over the years, Kathy has given them more books and materials as well as money for benches and tables.

The new library opened in February 2004 and proved to be so successful that the school authorities decided to erect a free-standing building in their compound to serve the students of the school as well as the community. Kathy agreed to share the costs by matching the funds they raised. Progress has been slow but already, the walls are up and the roof is on and students are enjoying the new facility.

KATHY IS THE FIRST TO RECOGNIZE THAT THESE SMALL INITIATIVES dotted around the country need constant encouragement if they are to succeed. On her twice-yearly trips to Ghana, she tries to visit as many of them as possible and brings her knowledge and new ideas to help teachers or librarians who are often working under difficult circumstances. This also gives her a chance to remind them, over and over again, about the importance of reading aloud to the children.

Everywhere she goes, the reception is always the same. Swarms of excited youngsters rush to greet her with a song of welcome or a specially-composed poem. In the rural communities, she starts off with a visit to the local chief. She then greets the staff and, as soon as the formalities are over, she picks up a book, sits down with the children and reads them a story. "*Once upon a time...*" she begins, and children add a chorus of "*time, time...*" and she continues.

"Children never tire of hearing a story," she says. "This is one of the best ways to stimulate their imagination. Sometimes I suggest to a child that they take a book, open it to any page and make up a story from this page. It's amazing what they come up with."

Each visit has its own flavour. I accompanied Kathy on a trip that took us to another library opening in Huni Valley, a village in the Western Region, where the whole town joined a parade of local chiefs who strolled into the compound with great pomp and ceremony. Towards the end of the program, Kathy stood before the gathering and taught the children how to sing and act out the song "*Head and shoulders, knees and toes,*" speeding up with each verse as the youngsters dissolved into giggles. She was reaching the final round of the song when a dignified grey-haired chief, clad in his colourful *kente* cloth sarong, was unable to contain his delight. Unabashed, he leapt to his feet and joined in the fun.

TRAVELLING AROUND GHANA TO VISIT DISTANT LIBRARIES IS ALWAYS A challenge. There are few trains, buses are slow and schedules unreliable while the roads are poorly maintained, always clogged by traffic—or by sheep or goats—and often become just barely passable. But nonetheless, a journey with Kathy is always a memorable experience, and I have shared dozens of them. She chooses to travel by car, even though she is always mindful of the fact that road accidents claim more lives in Ghana than all diseases put together.

She was on one of her visits to a rural library with volunteer Sally Irwin when their taxi broke down. The driver managed to fix the problem but within minutes, they realized, as they saw a thunderstorm approaching, that the doors of the van were stuck shut and the windows stuck open. When the deluge began, they also discovered that the windshield wipers were not functioning. Undeterred, Kathy moved to the front seat, grabbed a towel, leaned out of the front window and did her best to wipe the glass clear as they continued to drive along. Miraculously, they reached their destination safely.

Since Kathy met Kwame Katsekpor, she is more than happy to place her life in his hands. He is an excellent driver, suitably cautious and endlessly patient. His skill at navigating the Accra traffic allows her the chance to catch up on phone calls, book appointments and check up on already-booked appointments, even take a nap. On visits to distant libraries, she fills the trunk with books and games, puzzles and posters and a supply of drinking water. At every police check where the officials ask Kwame to open the trunk for inspection, Kathy jumps out of the car and, thanks to her commanding presence (and no doubt the colour of her skin), she manages to save him a few cedis.

Trips with Kathy could never be considered five-star travel. She is forever keeping a close eye on her budget so chooses accommodation at the most basic guesthouses—two, three, even four to a room, running water if you are lucky, washrooms down a darkened hall. She forgoes lunch and settles for take-outs from roadside stalls—the ever-popular roasted plantains and deep fried yams score the highest. When times get tough (and hot), Fan Yogo (frozen yogurt) works wonders. Always at the ready is a supply of granola bars brought from Canada.

Over the years, Kathy has covered every corner of the country—and well beyond. I joined her on a journey in 2009 that took us to Tamale, capital of the Northern Region. Setting out before dawn with Kwame on a road perpetually under construction, we drove the 200 kilometre stretch northwest to Kumasi, past dense plantations of palm, mango and banana trees, arriving by early afternoon.

Kumasi is Ghana's second city and, for three centuries, had been the seat of one of the most powerful kingdoms of West Africa. At its height, it covered an area that included most of modern Ghana, Togo to the east and the Ivory Coast to the west. It is still an important centre of Ghanaian culture and commerce and boasts what is reputedly the largest market in West Africa which snakes through the downtown area bringing traffic to a standstill.

The following morning, we pushed on another five hours to Tamale, northern Ghana's largest city, leaving behind the thick green forests and moving into the sparse and grassy savannahs and the dark red soil of the region. Parades of school children amble along the roadside, one they share with armies of cyclists balancing everything from firewood to metal pipes to small children on both front and back fenders. Here too in Ghana's North, Islam is the dominant religion so the piercing calls from the mosques are ever present.

A few kilometres outside the town where the road became little more than a dirt path, we reached the village of Wurishie. As the car pulled up to a low, concrete building, dozens of children rushed out waving their hands with excitement. A handsome young man, looking no older than 30, stepped forward and thrust out his hand to Kathy. "*Akwaaba, Akwaaba*", he said, engulfing her in a big hug. Razak Abdulrahaman has been the volunteer librarian of this small village venture since 2001 and he has performed miracles by turning the courtyard of his family compound into a small library that runs Monday to Friday afternoons. He uses every corner of the space to group the children according to their reading ability with a dozen of the smallest perched on stools in the far corner and the eldest on benches on the opposite side. All the others sit on a cement platform where they are shielded from the blistering sun by a canopy—built with a small grant from the Osu Children's Library Fund.

Kathy stepped to the front of the class and greeted the children. "Hello children. How are you?" "We are fine, thank you," they replied in sing-song unison. She then asked them about their favourite books and all hands shot up. *"Fly, Eagle, Fly,"* shouts one and another *"The Gingerbread Man."*

Kathy loves this connection with the children as they share their excitement over the books. The youngsters walk here from the surrounding villages every afternoon after school and it is clear they are captivated by the books and the stories. "All this happens because of Razak's leadership," says Kathy. "He gets paid nothing from his community but he carries on year after year for the children."

Kathy then fetched some of OCLF's "Library-in-a-Bag" gifts from the trunk of the car and ceremoniously presented them to the most deserving children. Before leaving, she handed out drinks and cookies and gave a farewell hug to Razak. "The dedication of this man is amazing," she says as she waved goodbye to the band of beaming children. "It is people like Razak that make our work so worthwhile."

The following day, we continued north to Bolgatanga ("Bolga" to the locals). Bolga is the northern-most town in Ghana, a short drive from the border with neighbour Burkina Faso. The region is strikingly different from the South. It is flat and dry, the hard-packed earth a dark red colour. In the distance, mud huts with pointed straw roofs like witch's hats huddle in circles among the few clusters of trees while all along the roadsides, fruit sellers stand hopefully behind pyramids of mangos and yams. To escape the heat, we joined a few locals in a nearby bar to sample a drink of *pito*, a type of beer made from fermented millet or sorghum and served in a calabash (a dried gourd).

It is in Bolga that Friends of African Village Libraries, a US-based NGO which works in partnership with OCLF, supports three libraries. We visited them all during the day, and at dusk, we stopped at one in Sumbrungu, a community on the edge of town. The library was housed in a room at one end of a partially-completed building. Since there was then no electricity, it closed down at night. The facility may be closed but the 'library' continued. At dusk, a parade of about 30 youngsters drifted into the compound. These are children whose school and family responsibilities take up most of the day so they are coming to this improvised evening class which provides their only chance to enjoy the books.

The children all sat on benches in the open courtyard, their small tables lit only by flickering candles. Darius, their earnest young librarian, helped them with homework, gave them writing exercises and read them stories.

Kathy sat on the sidelines watching the class. As the evening wore on and as night fell, she was wondering how the children got home at such a late hour and in the pitch dark. She needn't have worried. When the class ended at 10 p.m., Darius gathered the group together, grabbed his bicycle and prepared to walk each child to his home, some as far away as two kilometres. Kathy asked Darius if she could join him on his rounds. He agreed and the small escort team set out under a full moon. They delivered each child to his home, Darius hopped on his bike, signalled to Kathy to climb on the back fender and they rode home together. It was close to 11 p.m. when they reached the library.

"I'll remember that night as long as I live." says Kathy. "In so many of Ghana's villages, people like Razak and Darius are working with minimal resources and yet they are able to provide excellent instruction for so many village children."

Another library Kathy chose to visit on the same trip was miles from the nearest town. Wisdom of Wisdoms School is a tiny facility perched atop a small mountain in the Volta Region and within sight of the border with Togo, the country lying on Ghana's eastern border. Kathy had already donated books to this school's small library and the staff reported regularly on their progress so she decided to visit and offer more assistance.

The journey to the village of Kpoeta, the home of Wisdom of Wisdoms School, was a major challenge. The trunk of Kwame's taxi was packed with water and library supplies adding considerable weight to its human cargo. Kathy chose, as always, to sit in the back seat ("I feel safer there") as the car left the nearest town and bounced along a dirt road for almost an hour. The road eventually petered out and, as we climbed slowly upwards, it became a narrow deeply-rutted pathway with the shoulders on both sides eroded from the recent rains. More than once, Kwame veered to avoid the ruts, lurched to a near vertical angle and got stuck in the loose sand.

The minute we were finally in sight of the village, a large cluster of children spotted the car and began waving paper flags and singing a song of welcome. When we reached the top, head librarian Emmanual Tagbo stepped forward and, following local protocol, ushered us over to the 'chief's palace,' a sprawling, suburban-style bungalow. The chief wore his traditional finery, a brilliant yellow sarong made of the locally-woven *kente* cloth. He greeted Kathy with a smile and, through his interpreter, offered her a drink of Fanta. (An unopened bottle of vodka sat on the coffee table beside him, presumably a gift from a previous visitor.) Kathy was careful to observe the rules and not speak until spoken to, not to cross her legs in the chief's presence and not to offer her left hand. She explained her mission which was duly translated. The chief nodded in appreciation.

After the customary handshakes and farewells, Kathy led a procession of children back to the library courtyard and sat down beside a tiny one-room mud hut that carried the sign 'Explore with Reading' over the door. This was the village library. Inside were a few shelves of well-thumbed books and an ancient—and obviously idle—computer, presumably donated by some NGO. More than a hundred children sat outside, waiting patiently for a signal from their teacher to burst into song—first in English and then in French. Kathy greeted them and, with all eyes fixed on her, she asked the children to name their favourite books. Lots of little hands waved for attention. This time it was *Treasure Island* from one and *Yebo, Jamela!* from another.

She then gathered the staff around her to thank them for their efforts. As she does on all her visits, she encourages them to read to the children. "Read to them every day. Ask them questions about the story. Show them the title, the author's name. Ask them to make a story from each picture." A presentation of books and puzzles rounded out the visit and all the children waved her goodbye. They were still waving as the car threaded its way through the narrow laneway and back down the treacherous road.

Kathy continued waving from the back window of the taxi until the children were out of sight. "It is wonderful to see all that going on in such a tiny village so far from anywhere. And it shows that, with a tiny amount of money and a few books, you can make such a huge difference."

Kathy recently received an email from Emmanuel thanking her for the help she has given his library in the past and sharing some exciting news. "We want you to know that lives have improved, especially in our final examination results. Before the library, no one could make an 'A' in English but now many can and our school was awarded the best in the district."

ANOTHER TRIP TOOK US TO A VILLAGE A FEW KILOMETRES WEST OF Kumasi. Kathy had been invited by a Ghanaian friend, Patrick Agyemang, to stop by his village and advise him on the possibility of developing a library. But first, Patrick led us down the street to the chief's palace to pay our respects. The chief welcomed us warmly. He was an amiable man, dressed in a business suit rather than the traditional *kente* cloth wrap-around and he spoke movingly, in perfect English, about his family and about some of the concerns of his village.

He then asked Kathy what had brought her to his village. She told him about Patrick's library initiative and he appeared to be impressed. She went on to explain the importance of reading in a child's life, then asked him if he read to his own children. The chief hesitated for a moment, looked a little uncomfortable and said "well no," he didn't usually read to his children. "Well you should" said Kathy, wondering if she was being too forthright or breaching protocol. "If you read to your children, you would be setting an example to everyone in your village." Long pause. The chief looked a little taken aback, then nodded, placed his hand on his chest and replied "Thank you, Madam. You have given me much wisdom—here in my heart. I will do that."

Ghanaian board member Florence Adjepong is always amazed when she hears about another of Kathy's trips across the country. "I cannot believe her energy," she said. "She's seen more of the country than most Ghanaians and nothing is too much trouble. If it is going to help a community, a school, a library, she's going for it, no matter where it is. The word 'impossible' is simply not in her vocabulary."

She paused, then added "I often wonder if Kathy has any self-doubts about what she is doing. If she does, she certainly hides them well."

IN SPITE OF HER EVER-EXPANDING ENDEAVOURS IN GHANA, KATHY FINDS time to accept an increasing number of requests to visit other African countries. In 2007, the Save the Children Fund (USA) invited her to Mozambique, a country bordering South Africa and skirting the Indian Ocean. She spent a week giving workshops, visiting community libraries and sharing her ideas with teachers, development officers and government officials.

She followed the workshop in Mozambique with a return visit to neighbouring Zimbabwe. She had earlier attended the Zimbabwean International Book Fair in Harare, the capital, where she met an impressive young woman, Patricia Matira, who ran a library in the town of Marondera, an hour by bus from Harare. Kathy had often worried about Patricia as the situation in Zimbabwe deteriorated and she was anxious to meet her again and bring her some books and materials. Travel was uncertain in that unsettled country but Kathy managed to make the journey to Marondera lugging a large bag of library supplies.

Life was difficult for Patricia who was trying hard to keep her library open. After every rain, there was water dripping from the ceiling into buckets on the floor so she covered all the bookshelves with plastic to protect the books from the water. "There was simply no money for anything," Kathy recalls. "I just couldn't believe that Patricia and her staff could do so much with no money. But despite their tremendous hardships, she was doing a heroic job providing leadership for many children and fellow staff." Kathy has kept in touch with Patricia and invited her to Ghana in November 2012 to receive training from Joanna, visit all the OCLF libraries and to meet the staff and the children. Patricia called it "the most transforming experience of my life." During her two-week stay, she won many friends and carried back ideas and materials to share with her own library staff.

Kathy has also made three trips to Tanzania. Her first visit was in 2007 at the request of a Canadian donor to see if she could offer assistance to the Robin Hurt Wildlife Foundation (RHWF) which was supporting community development projects.

She flew first to Arusha in Tanzania, then travelled for 14 hours on treacherous roads, some they almost had to 'boat' across, to reach the RHWF camp. The school she visited had only a few books, all in English. Most had been supplied by well-meaning donors but had little relevance to these students who lived in such a remote corner of Tanzania and who spoke little English. Kathy did what she could to help the staff but she was asked if she could return to offer more help to this and to other communities.

Kathy returned to Tanzania later that year, this time with Joanna, to lead a three-day workshop for teachers and children from seven other schools in the same area. They brought with them several boxes of children's books including many written in Swahili. They also bought games and materials in Arusha, the nearest city, for the workshop. Again, Kathy spent time with the teachers while Joanna talked about books and gave each child and teacher the chance to write a story. They also handed out copies of another of Kathy's books, *One Little Crab*, which she had translated into Swahili.

It was during this trip that Kathy did the research and photography for two photo-illustrated books: *Maria's Wish* and *Peter's Wish*, books helping to address the serious concerns in the region of deforestation and poaching.

Kathy found these visits to such remote communities—somewhere vehicles had rarely reached—to be "the most humbling experience" and she was thrilled that Joanna was able to join her. "I see this as development in its purest sense, where people who live on the same continent have an opportunity to share with others who face similar problems. I like the idea of an African helping other Africans." She travelled to Tanzania again in 2010, this time offering a three-day workshop for students and staff from 14 Maasai schools in a different community. Each school received a trunk filled with Swahili storybooks as well as a few English books, along with supplies to mend them and plastic to cover them in the event of rain. In each case, this was the beginning of their school library.

Other African countries such as Cameroon, Togo, Burkina Faso, Kenya and Uganda have also benefited from Kathy's expertise. This could be in the form of library training for teachers and would-be librarians, book donations, funding for library furnishings or personal consulting visits. "More than anything else, it is my hope that the approach we have used in Ghana will help other developing countries. After all, it is really so simple."

## CHAPTER 18

# A Publishing Venture Takes Off

WHEN KATHY FIRST SET OUT ON HER LIBRARY MISSION, SHE COULD never have dreamed that her project would ultimately veer in a different, though not unrelated, direction. Nor would she have imagined that this new direction would perhaps be the most far-reaching of all her ventures.

It came about in a curious way. The more time Kathy spent visiting different schools, the more she realized that many of the students she encountered, even those who appeared to be good readers, had, in fact, very few literacy skills. They could read the words but they rarely understood what they were reading. So she devised a test to measure the children's reading skills and their ability to understand what they read. It was in 2000 that she launched her first comprehensive reading study.

The point of the study was to show that reading makes a difference to a child's performance in school and that the intervention of teachers is crucial. Thanks to a grant from the non-profit American Jewish World Service, she set to work. She gave her services for free but she needed money to buy book cabinets, reference books and storybooks for the schools which participated in the study. The Ghana Education Service (GES) endorsed the project heartily.

The first section of the study involved 200 students chosen from eight government schools in two districts of Accra. Kathy gave a book cabinet and a supply of books to six of the schools and asked the teachers to read aloud to the pupils every day and to allow time for independent reading. The study also expected students to organize journal writing once a week for the strongest readers. The remaining two schools had neither books nor teacher intervention and served as the control group.

Not surprisingly, the students in the group with the most intervention recorded the greatest improvement in their reading ability. The teachers were quick to notice too that stories they read to the students quickly became their favourites and that there was a direct correlation between teacher involvement and the opening up of the world of books. Ideally, by the end of the year, the teacher has read all the books in the box and had introduced every book to the students.

The second part of the study involved 230 students and the goal was to evaluate the books that had been previously supplied by the GES for their scheduled library periods. These were kept in large metal boxes in the head teacher's office. Jen Neufeld, a volunteer from Winnipeg, worked with Kathy evaluating each of the books for its reading level. They were both dismayed by what they found. It turned out that the GES had issued these boxes filled with books for the pupils but no one had checked to see if the books were suitable for that particular age group or for their reading level. In some cases, the books appeared to have never been opened.

When they evaluated the reading level of the students and checked the books that were available to them, Kathy and Jen found that there were very few books that the students in that particular class could read. The level of the books was much too high so they just remained in the box.

Most unfortunate of all was the fact that there were no books at all for the beginning reader. The youngest pupils would therefore never have the chance to take that important first step towards reading.

The outcome of the study was not unexpected. Not surprisingly, the group with the greatest teacher intervention, daily story time with the teacher and journal writing every week became the strongest readers. It was also clear that the books supplied by the government did not match the reading levels of the students.

The study provided an excellent tool to convey to the GES that positive intervention makes a significant difference to school grades and that the involvement of the teacher is of great importance.

It also signalled a critical need for books, especially for younger children and beginning readers—books which would catch their attention, would hold their interest and would hopefully turn them into readers. Even more important was the need for books that reflected the children's culture. "We were very aware of the difficulty finding books that were culturally relevant," said Kathy. "Books we were bringing from Canada were better than nothing but, no matter how hard we tried to send only ones that were relevant to African children, most of them still reflected the lives of white urban children and North American communities." Kathy decided it was time to address the problem.

SOON AFTER THE STUDY ENDED, A FRIEND GAVE KATHY A CATALOGUE of books published by Sub-Saharan Publishers, a local publishing company based in Accra and run by the formidable Akoss Ofori-Mensah, a handsome woman with a no-nonsense manner. Akoss is one of only a handful of female publishers in West Africa. Given the vagaries of publishing, especially in the developing world and more especially for women, it has not been an easy road. She has been a true and committed pioneer in her field.

Kathy sent Akoss an email to say she had seen her catalogue and hoped she would publish books for the very young reader. Akoss' immediate reply was "Have you any suggestions?"

Kathy recalled that she had once asked Lydia Tingan, one of the earliest library members who she has helped over the years, to tell her stories about growing up in a small village in northern Ghana. One she remembered was an encounter she had with a bee hive. Kathy shared the idea with Marty Helgerson, her neighbour in Winnipeg and a talented writer and the two set to work. Marty sketched out an outline of a story in a style suitable for early readers and one that was familiar to Ghanaian children and came up with a text which they called *Lydia and the Honey Tree*. Marty modelled the story on the highly successful series of books about Franklin the Turtle. "These were stories where everything turned out fine in the end. It worked for Franklin, so we used the same idea for our book"

They sent the story to Akoss who thought the text was good, but she felt they needed a more distinctly Ghanaian name that is more recognizable as one from northern Ghana. They chose the name Fati and their first book *Fati and the Honey Tree* was born. It was published jointly in 2002 by Sub-Saharan Publishers and the Osu Children's Library Fund. Ghanaian artist, Therson Boadu, provided the illustrations and, in 2006, he received the prestigious Toyota Children's Literature Prize for his drawings.

Two more Fati stories followed: *Fati and the Old Man* and *Fati and the Green Snake* based on more of Lydia's childhood experiences. A fourth story, *Fati and the Soup Pot*, is in the works. The first book, *Fati and the Honey Tree* has been translated into French and six Ghanaian languages while all three have been transcribed into Braille. "Kathy has very good instincts," said Marty. "She is almost always right and developing the Fati books was no exception."

The success of the Fati books has been remarkable. Almost overnight, children all over Ghana adopted Fati as their favourite storybook character, easily overtaking earlier favourites such as Cinderella and Snow White. Step into any classroom, in any corner of the country, and ask the children to name their favourite storybook character and the whole class will shout "FATI!"

Fati fans turn up everywhere. A young girl in Burkina Faso wrote to Kathy to tell her how much she loved the Fati books. "I love them because my life is exactly like hers (ma vie ressemble la sienne)," she wrote. Years after the publication of *Fati and the Honey Tree*, Kathy made a challenging overland journey from Accra to Timbuktu, in neighboulring Mali, with her daughter Akos and Lydia. They visited different schools on the way back and, at each one, Fati proved to be the most popular storybook character. When Kathy introduced Lydia as "the REAL Fati", the children cheered with delight.

On the same northern trip, the travellers made a detour to Wa, the regional capital of the Upper West Region of Ghana, to visit the Wa School for the Blind. Kathy had earlier sent them Braille copies of two of the Fati books and she was anxious to know how the children had responded to them. As she moved from one classroom to the next, she asked how many had read the Fati books. Nearly every hand went up. One of the older students even stood and proudly recited the whole book by heart.

Even though these students couldn't see the illustrations, they were just as enthusiastic about the books so the story obviously works on its own.

Years after the birth of Fati, I visited Akoss in her office atop a three-storey building in downtown Accra and found her sitting behind a cluttered desk, the walls covered with the many awards she has received. She dropped everything to welcome me and to discuss the state of publishing in Ghana.

"There have always been books imported from abroad but of course they reflected a totally different culture," Akoss acknowledged. "They were also very expensive so they were available to very few." It was in 1995, at a workshop on children's literature organized by the Children's Library Foundation that the children attending the workshop spoke out for the first time. They complained about the illustrations in books, that they were often inaccurate, that they were not very pretty and that they were not in colour. "It was important that these observations were coming from the children themselves," Akoss noted. "That really opened the eyes of publishers." Akoss pointed out that the technology for printing quality books in colour was still at an early stage in Ghana. "Printing in colour needed the right kind of paper and a more sophisticated technology. It just wasn't available in Ghana back then. Also, during the '70s and '80s, printing companies spent their time and money printing newspapers. They were seldom printing books."

Akoss went on to explain another roadblock to printing in Ghana. While Europeans put their traditions into writing hundreds of years ago, she explained, most of the African stories were oral and still remain so.

Publishers listened when the children spoke out at that 1995 workshop. Akoss herself took note. Soon after, she took two of her most popular books, *Sosu's Call* and *The Magic Goat,* which had been printed in black and white, and reprinted them in colour, becoming the first person in Ghana to publish children's books in colour. "People thought I was crazy. They also thought I had a lot of money. I didn't, but with technology inching ahead, I knew it was time to act."

KATHY HAD NO WAY OF KNOWING THAT THE BIRTH OF FATI WOULD signal the beginning of a new direction for the Osu Children's Library

Fund. "To write good stories which will catch the attention of children, you have to have a love for children and a gift for writing," says Akoss Ofori-Mensah. "You also have to have a taste for beautiful books. Kathy has all these—in abundance.

"Furthermore, Kathy and I both know that a good story is a way of preserving a culture, of teaching morals and passing on information. A story builds bridges between the young and the old. It provides a medium for sending out messages about issues such as crime and HIV/AIDS. And," she added, "they are good for character and confidence-building. And as you see so vividly in all Kathy's libraries, stories come alive when they are read and discussed."

WITH THIS STRONG ENDORSEMENT FROM ONE OF GHANA'S TOP PUBLISH-ers ringing in her ears, Kathy began to dream up more story ideas. She had discovered about this time that she had a real passion for photography. She started out as a virtual beginner and practised taking pictures everywhere she went—at neighbourhood street parties, at birthday gatherings or at celebrations for newborn babies. She spent a full afternoon at a woman's centre for low-income mothers and their children snapping pictures and made a print for each of her chosen subjects. All this practice gave her the confidence to use her newly acquired photographic skills and try her hand at photo-illustrated books for children.

Winnipeg photographer Bruce Hildebrand helped guide her first efforts and together, they created a simple alphabet book *A is for Ampe* (a popular jumping and clapping game played by young Ghanaian girls) and a numbers book *One Little Crab*. Each one carries a simple text and features photos of children from her libraries and familiar objects from their daily life—toys, animals, friends. Kathy then ventured out on her own to produce four colour books—*My Red Book, My Blue Book, My Yellow Book, My Green Book*. Three more followed later—*My Orange Book, My Violet Book* and *My Pink Book*. Then came a book of opposites, a book of shapes and, for the youngest reader, *All About Ama*, with pint-sized Ama pointing to her different body parts. The minute these books appeared on the library shelves, they were among the first to be snapped up. "The children just loved seeing themselves in the books," said Kathy. "When they see pictures of their own surroundings, it encourages them to learn the words. Even if they cannot read, they can look at the pictures and tell their own stories."

To find the best subject and the perfect shot, Kathy spends hours wandering through back streets, laneways and markets of Accra with her camera at the ready. She takes dozens of shots for each photo, usually early in the early morning or at the end of day when the sun is less intense. Back at the guesthouse, she transfers the photos onto her computer and files the best ones away, ready for another book.

Next came a series of four more books called *Literacy Changed my Life* made possible by a grant from the Hong Kong-based Chen Yet-Sen Family Foundation. For these, Kathy drew on real-life success stories from four students in the literacy classes—a hairdresser, a seamstress, a caterer and a welder. Thanks to their newly-learned reading and writing skills, they were better equipped for their trades. These books continue to provide inspiration for other literacy students as well as tools for teachers of English.

Another book sprang from the countrywide celebrations marking the 50th anniversary of Ghana's independence on March 6, 2007. On the day when Accra was awash with Ghana's red, yellow and green flags and vibrant costumes, Kathy visited a dozen different venues where she took hundreds of photos and produced a colourful record of the day called *Ghana@50*.

Some of Kathy's books have involved research in distant corners of the country. A series of three books featuring Ghana's natural resources included *David's Day at the Mine* which led her into a heavily-guarded gold mine in western Ghana to track the working day of David Mensah, a gold miner. Research for another, *Amoako and the Forest,* took place in the village of Mim, a lumber town in the Brong-Ahafo Region northwest of Kumasi. There, she followed Amoako who worked in the forestry industry and who showed her every detail of lumber production, from the felling of the trees to the creation of fine furniture. A visit to the Wechiau Community Hippo Sanctuary in the remote Upper West Region led to another book called *Mumaizu and the Hippos.* Tracking the elusive hippos was one challenge while another was sleeping in a 'hippo hide,' a tree platform with only a wobbly ladder between it and the ground.

One of Kathy's most ambitious book projects was a third book in the natural resource series called *Otu Goes to Sea*, one which was born in the seaside village of Goi. The book describes the daily life of Otu, a fisherman's son, who lives in the village which is also home of one of Kathy's libraries. Noreen Mian, the Canadian volunteer who was helping in Goi at the time, wrote the text while Kathy provided the photographs. Perfectionist that she is, she insisted that in order to get the best shots, she needed to join the fishermen when they headed out on their early morning run. They were skeptical at first, fearing that Kathy could not swim but they finally agreed, only if she was accompanied by the local assemblyman. She set out at dawn in a 20-foot-long fishing canoe with a boatload of fishermen and ten-year-old Otu.

Kathy spent five hours on the choppy seas, took many photos and returned to shore to a hero's welcome. Only later did she learn that this was the first time a woman had ever been allowed to join one of the fishing expeditions. Whenever she returns to Goi, she is warmly welcomed by the fishermen she joined that day.

KATHY HAS SO FAR PRODUCED 35 PHOTO-ILLUSTRATED BOOKS THAT HAVE reached many corners of Africa, including Sierra Leone, Liberia, Tanzania, Kenya, Uganda and Lesotho. Some have been translated into Kiswahili for readers in Tanzania, others into Dioula for children in Mali and Burkina Faso. Two have been translated into Spanish for schoolchildren in Peru while ten of her books are now available in Portuguese and are being distributed to preschools in rural Mozambique. The proceeds from her books sold in Ghana help provide funds for bonuses, health insurance and Christmas food parcels of rice, oil and sugar for library staff—the small but important items that the government doesn't provide.

What Kathy's books have clearly highlighted is the importance of books that are relevant to the African children's lives. Paulette Bourgeois, author of the popular *Franklin the Turtle* series of children's books, travelled to Ghana in November 2010 to host a workshop for would-be writers. One afternoon, she dropped into the Osu Library where the children had prepared a special treat in her honour: they would act out a short play based on one of her books, *Franklin Has a Sleepover.* Two children dressed up, one as Franklin the Turtle and the other as his friend Bear.

As the story unfolded, Paulette noticed that very few of the children appeared to follow the simple story of Franklin inviting Bear to his house to spend the night. At the end of the story, when Bear says that he hopes next time Franklin will come to his house for a sleepover, Franklin is thrilled and does his 'happy dance.' With those two words, the drums struck up, the children jumped to their feet and began to dance around the compound. "I realized sitting there that a sleepover is completely foreign to those children," said Paulette. "They probably sleep together all the time. It was only at the words 'happy dance' that they got it!" It was a stark reminder that not all books strike recognition in all children.

Kathy's most recent publishing project has added another dimension to her mini book industry. In 2007, she hired Edmund Opare, a gifted Ghanaian artist, to illustrate two of her latest books. These stories were originally written by Angela Christian, a Ghanaian woman who gave the texts to Kathy years ago in the hope that she could help her find a publisher. Kathy tried to act but, in the meantime, Christian died. Given that Kathy was now her own publisher and still had Angela's manuscripts, she sought the family's permission to rewrite and publish the two stories. The first, *Kente for a King,* features Edmund Opare's striking and colourful illustrations. The second, *Akosua's Gift,* tells about a young Ghanaian girl who makes a clay water pot as a gift for her sister's wedding. The book, also illustrated by Opare, was listed as one of four 'notables' by the 2011 Children's Africana Book Award committee.

"Working with Kathy has been a revelation for me," said Edmund, a quiet and gentle man. "She is one of the few people I have met who has such a passion for what she is doing. She is so calm you always feel comfortable in her presence. Also, she listens more than she talks. That is very rare."

KATHY'S SEARCH FOR MATERIAL FOR MORE CHILDREN'S BOOKS HAS even taken her beyond the borders of Africa. Ever since she spoke at a conference in Hong Kong promoting libraries for development, she had been intrigued by the idea of visiting rural China and creating books for rural Chinese children. She had hoped to receive support from a Chinese foundation but when this did not materialize, she decided to go anyway, at her own expense.

She set out for China in January 2009 and arrived in Shanghai unconcerned that it was the start of Chinese New Year when the whole country of more than 1.8 billion people was on the move. She continued on to Kunming where she arrived clutching the name and cell phone number of her only contact, a woman named Cecilia who was involved with a small NGO called the Smiling Library project.

Cecilia met her in Kunming and they travelled together by bus to Pu'er City to celebrate Chinese New Year with Cecilia's parents. The next day, they continued on, first by bus, then by motorbike to Plum Village in the rural countryside where Kathy was to stay with a family for the next ten days.

No one in the family spoke English and Cecilia had to leave soon after their arrival. However, Kathy relied on a basic sign language and managed to take enough pictures for three small books: a book of numbers, called *One Little Duckling* and *A Book of Opposites,* both patterned on her earlier English versions, and another called *Busy Baolin* for the youngest readers. The name Kathy Knowles was impossible to transcribe into Chinese so the author assumed the name 'Lily Chen.'

At the end of her stay, Kathy took a five-hour bus ride back to Kunming where she met up with Cecilia. She insisted on giving Kathy a tour of the city, produced a bicycle for her and the two took off. Cecilia navigated the crowded roads effortlessly but Kathy had to struggle to keep up. "It was the most harrowing experience trying to follow her," she said. "The traffic was horrendous, especially on the roundabouts. I was terrified I would lose her but I just tried to keep an eye on her broad-brimmed hat." Cecilia wrote to Kathy later that "I lost my bicycle, parked down the stairs of my apartment. So now I take bus every day. Safer by bus now. I won't risk my life on bike."

When the Chen Yet-Sen Foundation saw the book files, they agreed, in partnership with an initiative called Green Kids, to publish all three books with an English text and a Mandarin translation in the back and to distribute them freely to 150 rural Chinese schools in Yunnan.

IN 2010, WHEN KATHY ATTENDED THE INTERNATIONAL CONGRESS of IBBY (International Board on Books for Young People) in Spain, she had met Jocelyne Trouillot, a professor from Université Caraïbe, a small university in Port-au-Prince, capital of Haiti. Earlier that year, the country had been devastated by a serious earthquake which flattened towns, schools and hospitals, killing thousands and leaving even more homeless. Subsequent rain storms and a cholera epidemic also took their toll.

Jocelyne had already seen Kathy's books and asked her if she could create some for the children in Haiti, using a text in Creole, their language, and featuring children from Haiti. There are so many children in need, especially after the earthquake, she pointed out, and there are only a few books in Haitian Creole.

The following March, Kathy travelled to Haiti with Sally Irwin, her friend and OCLF volunteer, to photograph Haitian children for two books. On her arrival in Port-au-Prince, she was stunned to find that the five-storey university that Jocelyne and her husband had built some years before had been almost completely demolished by the earthquake, killing 40 of its students and staff. Determined to keep the university running, they had erected a few aluminium-roofed rooms, no bigger than ten by ten feet, where the remaining students could gather.

Kathy visited two schools to seek out suitable subjects for her books. She was saddened to see many children looking tired and hungry and learned from one teacher that those in kindergarten often arrived without breakfast and are given only one meal a day, usually in the evening. "There were tents all over the capital providing homes for those who had lost their houses in the quake. But the charm and beauty of Haiti shone through the damage and it was a privilege to be there."

During her brief stay, Kathy took enough pictures for two books. One she called *Beauty* (inspired by the photographer Annie Leibovitz) and it showed pictures of different objects the children found beautiful— a flower, a cow, a fish. In the other, called *On My Way to School,* she followed the daily routine of young Misoule as she prepared for school:

collecting water, bathing, dressing, brushing her hair. Both books included a text in Creole. Kathy had hoped to finish a third book but the day before her departure, there was an anticipated announcement of the presidential election results and violence was expected. "I was rushing around to see if I could get the last few shots but it was just impossible and too dangerous." When Jocelyne received copies of the first books, she was thrilled and wrote to Kathy "You have made such a beautiful present for the Haitian children. Thousands of thanks. Jocelyne."

UNTIL 2009, KATHY PUBLISHED ALL HER BOOKS IN CANADA, PHOTO-shopping each image on her computer, transferring the photos and text to a disc or uploading them to her computer and sending the file to Friesens printers south of Winnipeg to complete the job. Given her penchant for perfection, she always travels the 100-kilometre journey to their factory to personally supervise every step of the production. She then faces the challenge and expense of shipping the finished books over to Ghana. As often as possible, she seeks out willing travellers to carry some of the boxes or saves them for the rare occasion when she commissions a shipping container.

She was still publishing her books in Canada when a fortuitous meeting with Gibrine Adam, head of Ghana's EPP Books Services, the largest book distribution company in West Africa, opened up new possibilities. Gibrine is not only a very successful book publisher and distributor but he is a former primary school teacher and a savvy bookseller. He therefore has firsthand knowledge of the community he serves.

Gibrine is a suave and debonair gentleman who stands more than a head taller than Kathy. He took an instant shine to her as well as to her books and agreed to publish and distribute anything she gave him. It was music to her ears. Now that EPP has developed the technical skill and has acquired the materials to print high-quality paperback books in colour and in Ghana, Kathy has entrusted EPP with the publishing of five of her titles. The results were not totally to her satisfaction but it was an encouraging start.

"I like to support Kathy because I believe in what she does," says Gibrine, sinking his 6'6" body into a large leather couch. "She is such a selfless person who loves and supports children and education. I'm trying to do the same thing by donating ten percent of our books free to needy schools. What is also important is that Kathy pays attention to every single detail and that helps us keep our standards high.

"The response to her books has been tremendous," he continued. "So many kids identify with them, especially those in the rural areas. They look at those wonderful pictures and say 'that could be my brother or my sister.' Or 'that looks like my village.' That is so helpful in getting kids to read."

Now that Kathy has established a fruitful working relationship with EPP Books Services, she hopes to have more of her books printed in Ghana which will not only help boost Ghana's economy but will solve the enormous headache of transporting them across the Atlantic. With EPP on side, her books already appear in dozens of outlets around Ghana. If Gibrine's ambitious plans to expand into other West African markets should materialize, her books may soon find their way into bookstores further afield.

KATHY IS THRILLED BY THE POSITIVE RECEPTION TO HER BOOKS, BOTH in Ghana and in Canada. When she's not worrying about her bank balance or her staff salaries or the leaking roofs, she is dreaming up more ideas for more books. "It is our libraries that provide the inspiration for most of our books," she says. "I know the children well so they are my best subjects. I can tell when I watch them looking at these books that they see themselves in those pages and it is clear that this helps them build self-esteem and confidence. Ultimately, this also helps them to become readers and, after all, that's our real aim, isn't it?"

## CHAPTER 19

# Challenges and Rewards

ANYONE WHO EVER DOUBTED THAT KATHY HAS A LIFE APART FROM building libraries, reading to children and writing books may be surprised to learn that, in spite of the 14 hour days she puts in, both in Canada and in Ghana, she somehow manages to squeeze in time with her family and seizes every opportunity to skate, ski, cycle, and run marathons with one or all of them. As her 50th birthday loomed in 2005, she decided to mark the occasion by signing up, with her son Alastair, then age 18, for the first ever Africa-based Ironman triathlon. This gruelling event involves a 3.8 kilometre swim, followed by a 180 kilometre cycle, followed by a full 42.2 kilometre marathon run, all in one day. Most people in the world are unaware of this race, but thousands participate at the various venues held on different continents every year.

Kathy knew that this would be a huge challenge but she was determined to give it a try. Six months before the big day, she cancelled her car insurance and spent two hours every day cycling indoors or running outside even when Winnipeg's winter weather dipped below minus 30 degrees. On alternative evenings, she ran to the nearest pool and swam one hundred lengths.

Alastair was travelling and in late March, they managed to meet up in Port Elizabeth on the southern coast of South Africa where they joined hundreds of athletes gathering for the event. She wasn't intimidated to find that most of the other participants were seasoned Ironman racers, clad in spiffy spandex outfits and riding top-of-the-line bicycles. Kathy wore simple bike shorts and a tank top and rode a basic 18 speed cycle. She appeared unconcerned about how and when to shift gears, and nonchalant about the fact that she didn't even know how to change a tire.

The first day's practice run was a bitter test. She almost changed her mind when she saw the size of the gigantic waves. "When I saw those waves, I honestly began to wonder if I was ready for this, in spite of all the training," she admitted. She had even more doubts during the practice swim when she suddenly came close to what she thought was a shark. "That really freaked me out though I think it must have been a dolphin. I really began to think 'am I crazy to be doing this?'"

The following morning, at 7 a.m. sharp, the competitors gathered at the beach. Kathy and Alastair were among them, standing nervously at the ready. "On the day of the event, there is a really exhilarating feeling that you are part of something that is much bigger than yourself. All I could do was to give it my best." At the sound of the starting gun, Alastair shouted "I love you Mum" and they both dashed into the open sea for the 3.8 kilometre swim. Kathy finished the swim ahead of Alastair, then ran to shore, changed into her shorts and shirt, pinned on her bib number 214 and mounted her bike. She completed the 180 kilometres of the cycle section in good time and thought to herself "I'm okay now. I know I can make it."

But the most gruelling part lay ahead—the 42.2 kilometre run, a full marathon. She acknowledged that this was by far the toughest section. At one point, she found she couldn't walk in a straight line and was getting very cold, possibly the effects of hypothermia. She picked up a jacket from a volunteer and continued walking, by now in the pitch dark. She found it eerie walking alone in the dark but, at some point, a young boy appeared on a bicycle and he stayed with her and urged her on. Further along, she stopped to use a port-a-potty. "My body ached so much and I was so cold I could hardly lower myself onto the seat!"

Once she was in sight of the finish line, she started to run "in my own feeble way" and when she finally staggered across the finishing tape, she fell into the arms of a welcoming Alastair. She was one of the oldest women to participate in the race, but she managed to arrive just after 11:30 p.m. to a cheering crowd and a fluttering Canadian flag. She finished in 16 and a half hours after setting out that morning and only a scant half hour after her 18-year-old son.

Kathy is the first to acknowledge that it had been a tough race but that didn't stop her from entering another Ironman event three years later, this time in Lanzarote, one of the Canary Islands. Once again, she took on a serious exercise routine to prepare for the event. Even in Ghana, she managed to maintain her training schedule, though this often proved perilous. On her last day in Ghana, hours before she was leaving for the airport, she was running in the dark when it was cooler, tripped and fell into a gutter damaging one of her legs. She taped up the leg for the journey home and was back on her feet within a week, eager to restart training for the challenge ahead.

Lanzarote is considered by the professionals to be the most difficult race of all the Ironman courses due to the island's strong headwinds and steep uphill climbs. One was an 18 kilometre ride up a slope that circled upwards and around a volcano. This time, at 52, Kathy was one of only eight women competitors over 50. "Sure it was tough, but it was also beautiful as we biked beside large lava fields and swam among tropical fish." This time, she made it to the finish line by 11:49 p.m., 11 minutes after Alastair. A week later, she flew to Ghana.

KATHY'S SENSE OF ADVENTURE IS STILL THERE, AS IT ALWAYS WILL BE. On her April 2012 trip to Ghana, she stopped to visit the Bologna Children's Book Fair en route. After the fair, she had a few days to spare before her flight to Accra so she rented a bicycle and cycled alone some 300 kilometres south along the Adriatic coast. She was hardly deterred by an unfamiliar cycle with gears she had trouble mastering, nor by the trucks and cars that sped past her, nor by the steep uphill climbs (no shoulders) sometimes measuring several kilometres. One day, she rode 130 kilometres, many of them uphill, to reach her destination. "Some of it was a bit scary," she acknowledged. "The hills seemed to get bigger and bigger and, at one point, sweat was dripping off my face so I got off and walked." She then decided to return to Bologna by train and somehow managed to locate the train station, buy a ticket and board a train (with bicycle) for the return journey—all with little more than a few words of Italian.

THERE IS NO DOUBT THAT KATHY WILL CONTINUE TO TRAVEL FAR AND wide, to take on challenges that would flatten most, to assume risks in the face of skeptics and to accomplish more in a day than most people do in a week. Although her work in Ghana has not been as physically taxing as an Ironman competition or a cross-country bike ride, the challenges have been legion. She did it because of her deep affection for the children of Ghana and her dogged determination to improve their lives. "If you want to know what drives me," she once said, "it is simply the innate desire to help. When you start helping others, you realize your own capacity to give, to make a difference, a really meaningful difference. And it always feels good to give."

People often ask what would happen to her 'baby' if, for any reason, she was no longer able to run it. She pauses for a few seconds, then offers a measured reply. "Since we have always fought to have our library staff placed on the government payroll, I feel confident that the libraries would continue. Granted, there would be no way they could initiate new programs without the fundraising I do in Canada but I feel certain that the libraries that are now in place are firmly established and well staffed and they would continue. After all, the ideal for all development projects is that the donor could eventually withdraw and the project would continue. That's what I've always strived for."

It would be hard to count the number of lives Kathy has touched during her long mission in Ghana. There are the children she has rescued from poverty or from abusive situations. There are the ones she has carried to hospital in the middle of the night and those she has visited in prison. There are the families she has comforted at a time of bereavement, the numbers of children she has helped to finish school or to continue their studies. And there are the thousands upon thousands of youngsters who, thanks to her, have discovered the excitement of books and the magical world that is found in their pages.

What encourages her most is to see the children who have grown up in her library communities stepping out into the world and making a difference. The first six children who sat reading under the Flamboyant tree in her garden are shining examples. Philip is now a teacher and Becky has worked as an assistant teacher while pursuing a university degree. George has a job as a security guard at the British High Commission, and Richmond graduated from the Institute of Public Service and is working as a marketing manager for a private company. He also hopes to open a small library in New Adenta, his home on the edge of Accra, which he calls "my way of giving back." "If it wasn't for you and your family," he wrote to Kathy "I would never have acquired the habit of reading. Thank you for the motivation you gave me when I was young. I hope I am living up to my commitment by bringing a library to my community." Kathy beams with pride. "This is the biggest indicator of our success."

Kathy hears often from children who have benefited from her libraries and they are not shy about singing her praises. An email reached her recently from Rafiatu, a young woman who had visited the library in Osu in 1995 and has never forgotten the experience. She came from a very poor family and finding books to read was impossible. "Then I discovered your library and I was one of the happiest children you can ever imagine. It was like I had discovered gold."

Thanks to the library, Rafiatu learned to read and reached a level "as high as those in private and expensive schools." She worked hard to pay her way through university and graduated with a degree in sociology. "I want to say God bless you madam for letting an underprivileged kid like me have such an opportunity." Rafiatu has now returned to her village and has launched a project making and selling beads as a means of raising funds to give the girls in her village a chance to further their education.

Kathy is heartened when young Ghanaians show an interest in carrying on her work. "Most of all, I want these projects to last long after I am gone. I want them to be run entirely by Ghanaians, not by a Canadian woman from Winnipeg." She paused, then added "I often think that if young people are nourished both physically and emotionally, they will eventually become enlightened voters and will want the same from their leaders."

Already, there are encouraging signs that this is happening. One shining example is Deborah Ahenkorah, who visited the Kathy Knowles

Community Library as a young child in its early days. In June 2008, Deborah wrote to Kathy: "When I discovered your little container library, it was like paradise! Thank you for having added such joy to my childhood. All of those books I read opened my eyes to a wealth of experiences and made me aspire to bigger and greater things. My dream in future is to build libraries across Africa and to influence education and literacy in Africa. I have already begun to make this dream a reality." Deborah, now in her mid-20s and recently graduated from Bryn Mawr College in Pennsylvania where she had been awarded a scholarship, has made an admirable start. In 2008, she wrote dozens of proposals and appeal letters to raise the necessary funds to launch the first Golden Baobab Prize for African children's literature. In its first year, the competition for the prize drew more than one hundred entries. A story by Vivian Amanor, OCLF's librarian in Goi, was shortlisted for the prize and was one of the few winners from Ghana. The prize is now into its fourth year and is already helping to nurture a whole generation of African writers.

## CHAPTER 20

# A Lasting Legacy

ONE AFTERNOON IN APRIL 2010, WHEN KATHY AND I WERE NUDGING our way through the crowded market in downtown Accra, a call came through on a crackling cell phone line. The Osu Children's Library Fund, we were told, had been chosen to receive a prestigious award given every two years by the International Board on Books for Young People (IBBY), a world-wide organization promoting literacy among children. The aim of the award, the caller explained, was "to inspire and encourage all those working to bring children and books together—often in the most difficult circumstances." As an added bonus, it carried a cash price of $10,000 donated by the Japanese newspaper, *Asahi Shimbun*.

When we returned to the guest house, we were able to learn more about the prize. It seemed that the board's six-person international jury used the following criteria to make their selection:

Is the project sustainable?

Does it provide a framework for growth?

What is the impact of the project?

Is it original and innovative?

Can it provide a model for others?

Is it easily replicated?

Are any printed materials available?

The jury chairperson, Hannelore Daubert, reported that the jury had agreed that "with energy, commitment and a unique combination of visionary ideas and practical implementation, this organization (the

Osu Children's Library Fund) is encouraging and sustaining a reading culture in West Africa." The jurors went on to note that "the project instils in children, even the smallest, the joy of reading and in doing so enriches their self-esteem and will help to broaden their horizons. Not only children are taught reading and writing skills, but adults and teens, who have never had this opportunity, are encouraged to join the reading program, thus giving them confidence and a better chance in the job market."

We were stunned—and delighted—by such a positive endorsement of Kathy's relatively small organization. To think that it all began just over twenty years ago when an ordinary young woman from Canada, a mother of four with no library training, sat down with six children under a tree and read them a story. And that this modest beginning would eventually lead to the transformation of thousands of lives in far-away Africa.

Buoyed by the approval from such an important international organization, Kathy, Joanna and I set out that September to accept the award. By a stroke of good fortune, it was to be presented at the organization's 32nd congress which would be held that year in the Spanish city of Santiago de Compostela, well-known as the final destination of an 800 kilometre pilgrimage across northern Spain.

To fully appreciate the chosen location for the Congress, we decided to first walk a section of the route known as the Camino. We all strung a scallop shell around our necks—the mark of a true pilgrim— and walked the last 127 kilometres of the trail ending up at the ancient Cathedral of Saint James. Joanna was especially proud to learn from officials that it was the first time they had met anyone from Ghana who had ever walked the Camino.

The awards ceremony took place on the second last night of the congress when the 600 delegates gathered in the 15th century Hostal dos Reis Católicos built as a hospital for pilgrims, now a five-star Parador and one of the grandest hotels in Spain. We entered through a massive baroque doorway into what had once been the hospital's chapel where the ceremony was to take place. Satoshi Hashimoto, the representative of *Asahi Shimbun*, mounted the podium and introduced the winners.

Joanna, the first to speak, was visibly shaking as she stood before a roomful of delegates from around the world. Here was a young woman who had left her small village just 22 years before, travelled 150 kilometres to Accra and found work as Kathy's housekeeper. By swift stages, she ran Kathy's first tiny library, then her own much larger one before gradually moving ahead to oversee the whole network of OCLF libraries. She had never spoken before an audience of this size in her life, and here she was, on the stage in Spain, speaking to 600 book-lovers from around the world.

"I started working as house help for Kathy's family when they lived in Ghana," she said, clutching a lace handkerchief that was already soaked with perspiration. "I have shared the joy of reading with thousands of children and have taught others to do the same. Some of those children are now university graduates in the fields of medicine, banking and journalism. Parents often return to express their gratitude that our library played a significant role in their child's life." She paused, looking embarrassed, as the audience gave her a standing ovation.

Kathy was so moved by Joanna's words that she, like many in the room, was already wiping away tears. As she stood to speak, her voice cracking audibly, Joanna moved in behind her and, quite spontaneously, placed her arms around Kathy's waist. Kathy dabbed her eyes, then spoke. "Working with Joanna has been one of my life's greatest gifts, and accepting this award together is a great honour for us," she said, still struggling to hold back tears. "It is a privilege to have played a part in this library project, helping one child at a time enter the wonderful world of books. This prize money will help us continue to meet this goal."

TODAY, MORE THAN TWENTY YEARS AFTER KATHY OPENED THE DOORS of her first small library in her garage, the seven community libraries she has helped build in Accra have become well-used and greatly valued landmarks in the capital. Better still, local government authorities have at last begun to acknowledge the importance of these well-built and well-run facilities: as of December 2012, they have shown their approval by placing a total of 40 OCLF staff members on the government payroll, including 23 women. In a further vote of confidence, the previous year, all OCLF staff received small but significant pay raises.

Outside observers who have watched the project develop over the years strongly endorse the views handed down by the IBBY judges. Richard Beattie, a former senior officer with the Canadian International Development Agency (CIDA), has followed the growth of OCLF from its earliest days. He points out that, right from the beginning, Kathy has embedded her programs in the community. "When the idea for a new library is beginning to take shape in her head, she seeks the advice of community members to find out what they would like to see; what are their most important needs—a computer lab, wheelchair ramps, urinals or flush toilets, a study space for older students." Indeed, long before she commissioned the drawings for the library near the community of Madina, Kathy met with teachers from the local schools to hear their ideas and draw from their experience. Likewise in Nima, where her most successful initiatives—the thriving theatre company, the popular literacy classes, even the girls soccer team—all sprang from a real need expressed by community members.

Richard also notes that much of OCLF's success stems from the organization's strong support base in Canada. Thanks to around 350 loyal donors, largely in Canada, Kathy managed to raise around $350,000 in 2012. "It is highly unusual for a small organization to raise that sort of money with almost no government support," says Richard. "This frees her from the complicated application and reporting procedure that government agencies require and it therefore allows her a degree of freedom and flexibility."

Important too, notes Richard, is the strong support that Kathy receives from volunteers, especially those helping in Canada. The fact that her Canadian arm is run entirely by volunteers who have pitched in regularly for years, the fact that she takes no salary herself and that she locates her 'office' in the top floor of her Winnipeg home, she has managed to keep her administrative and fundraising costs to a remarkably low one to two percent compared to other charities where this figure often climbs well upwards from ten percent. "More and more, donors respect a charity that keeps these running costs down," says Richard. "They don't want their gift to be spent on salaries and stamps."

Most important of all, Richard emphasizes that Kathy has always ensured that what she has created is sustainable, by keeping it rooted in the local culture and hinged to local government budgets. The training programs run by Joanna for lay librarians help pass on her expertise to others. The literacy classes, once run by expatriates, are now largely taught by Ghanaians. Above all, the fact that Kathy has gone to great lengths to involve local government and hold them to their promise of paying staff salaries has won the admiration—and envy—of many observers. All those visits to the mayor's office, to the local assembly members, to the A.M.A have helped ensure that OCLF staff members will continue to be paid and that the water and power will continue to be supplied even after she withdraws. Says Richard: "This is what sustainability is all about. There are development programs that honour this principle in theory but are not prepared to take the time—or have the patience—to make it happen. When they leave the country, everything falls apart."

Richard's views are shared by Darren Schemmer, Canada's High Commissioner to Ghana from 2007 to 2010, who followed the work of the OCLF closely during his three-year tenure. "Many organizations die with their founder since that partnership with the government hasn't been firmly established," he said. "But Kathy has always ensured that the government is on side, no matter how difficult that may be. That gives local authorities a vested interest in the project, making it likely to continue, even after she is gone."

Reporting to donors is also an important part of sustainability. Kathy is fully aware that donors want to know how their money is spent so she keeps them up-to-date on all developments. "She does this very well," says Schemmer. "Since she has kept her organization relatively small, it is fairly easy for her to tell the story of her libraries. Donors want to see the results, they want to see the books on the shelves, the children reading and not feel that their money has gone into a big pot. Results can be more difficult to convey for larger organizations."

Darren Schemmer also noted on his visits to OCLF libraries how they had become gathering places for the community where people can meet and chat and learn, a little like the village water pump. "So many things emanate from those libraries," he said. "Just look at all the things that have flowed from that small blue shipping container." Schemmer's wife, Heather Johnston, who was also a stalwart supporter of the OCLF project during their Ghana posting, adds: "Kathy's influence, not only through her libraries but also through her books, is spreading all around Africa, and now to China, even to Haiti. She has planted many little seeds that will continue to spread long after she has left Ghana."

Beth Cramer, a librarian and Associate Professor at Appalachian State University in North Carolina, spent a month in Ghana in 2010 researching her doctoral thesis on the topic "International Library Development in Africa: Benefits, Challenges and Sustainability." She returned from Ghana hugely impressed by how the Osu Children's Library Fund functions, especially in terms of avoiding dependency. "The fact that Kathy is engaging people from the community to train the librarians and to run the libraries, the fact that she is now buying many of her books from a local publisher, the fact that she is inspiring educators and encouraging teachers, all this helps to avoid that dependency."

OCLF Board member Florence Adjepong, an educator herself who has seen the libraries grow since the days when she took her own children to the garden library, agrees. "Kathy's libraries are now all essentially running themselves with excellent, well-trained staff who have learned so much from her and who are now passing that expertise on to others. And furthermore," she adds, "what she has developed in Ghana is a model for community libraries everywhere, not only for Ghana but for anywhere in the developing world. It is a model which is community friendly, is easily maintained and which is transferable to any country or community, no matter how poor they are, no matter how little space they have. She has shown the way. And it works!

"I am reminded of the name of Maria Montessori, the Italian educator, who became synonymous with a system of childhood education that spread all over the world. I believe that in future, the name of Kathy Knowles will be synonymous with children's libraries everywhere."

VERY LITTLE OF THIS COULD HAVE BEEN DONE, WITH THIS AMOUNT OF success, in a country—such as many in Africa—where its people face ongoing internal conflicts or political suppression. Clyde Sanger, a former

Africa correspondent for *The Guardian* who lived and worked in both East and West Africa, suggests that this is an important factor in the sustained success of OCLF. "Kathy," he says, "walked into her garden with a basket of books at just the right moment in Ghana's political history. It was the precise period when the country's efforts to consolidate democracy and regain national pride were beginning to bear fruit."

Ghana, he recalls, lived through a long period of upheaval and a series of military coups following the demise of its founder, Kwame Nkrumah. But by the early 1990s, the time when Kathy began her library project, civil society began to blossom.

This political stability has continued to grow and has helped the country in many ways, not least economically. The discovery of oil in the 21st century is expected to provide jobs and income for some, though it will require skilled management to prevent the high level corruption that the presence of oil brought to Nigeria. While many people are expected to benefit from this discovery, a huge proportion of the country still lives well below the poverty line and it is this group that Kathy continues to serve.

Ghana's slowly developing democratic recovery was put to the test in the summer of 2012. On July 24, news broke to a stunned nation that their president, John Attah Mills, died suddenly in the local Military Hospital. He was just 68 and was expected to run in a forthcoming election five months away.

Within hours of the announcement, parliamentarians were summoned to witness the swearing in of the vice-president, John Dramani Mahama as president. The atmosphere was somber, respectful and dignified. As the new president stood to take his oath of office, he spoke movingly about his friend. "This is the saddest day in our nation's history," he said. "I am personally devastated. I have lost a father, I have lost a friend, I have lost a mentor, I have lost a senior comrade." He referred to his late friend as "Asumdwoehene", meaning 'prince of peace' in the Twi language.

John Mills had run unsuccessfully for president in 2000 and 2004 for the National Democratic Congress party (NDC). In 2009, he won a narrow victory, having been elected with a margin of less than one percent. The fact that the very close victory did not set off an explosion of violence, as had occurred in similar election results in Kenya and the Ivory Coast, was an indication of the strength of the country's democratic institutions.

Another election was held in December 2012 and the NDC, under the leadership of John Dramani Mahamna, won a narrow victory. It was a peaceful transition which international observers hailed as "another transparent vote in Ghana's history."

IT IS EARLY DECEMBER 2012, AND ANOTHER HOT, STEAMY DAY IN ACCRA. Once again, Kathy is nearing the end of her twice-yearly, five-week visits. The scenario is always the same as her departure looms: clutching her lengthy 'to-do' list, she is checking off all her last-minute chores: update her bank signature; add four new staff members to the government payroll; pick up a Canadian flag to replace the ragged one at the Nima Library; buy more flowering plants for the garden at Madina; take more photos for her newest book.

She is still packing her suitcase when driver Kwame arrives. Worried about the traffic, he is anxiously checking his watch. With farewell hugs to the landlady and anyone who happens to be passing by, she climbs in the car and heads for the airport with Joanna and Jennifer, her loyal send-off team. It is only when she has sunk into her seat on the plane that she is finally able to relax.

Each time the plane takes off after another of her visits to Ghana, Kathy finds herself thinking back to that tiny circle of six children who sat under the Flamboyant tree in her garden listening to her stories. Though their house on Osu Avenue has now been demolished and replaced by a row of townhouses, the spirit that was nurtured in that garden continues.

Today, there are men and women who can say with pride, 'I can read,' who can write a cheque, sign their name. Today, there are more books than ever that reflect the African children's culture. And everywhere there is a growing awareness of the importance of reading among teachers and educators, among parents and even among children.

Now, more than 20 years later, thanks to the libraries Kathy has built all over Ghana, as well as those she has supported in a half a dozen other corners of Africa, and in Haiti, in China and the Philippines, there is a generation of children growing up with books in their hands and storybook characters swirling around their heads. Long after she has gone, she will be fondly remembered each time a child turns the page of a favourite book. It is indeed a lasting legacy.

But Kathy is not one to rest on her laurels. She still remains deeply committed to her work even though she is reaching her late fifties—a time when many people start to fantasize about retirement. Not so Kathy. There are still thousands more children waiting for the chance to open their first storybook.

As she wings her way back to Canada, she is already unrolling the drawings for a new library to be built in Korle Gonno, another impoverished community in Accra next to the Nanka Bruce Junior High School and one that will serve a large and deprived fishing community. All the necessary permits are in order and the workmen have already started to dig. The new library will be on three levels, complete with a storytelling corner, a theatre and a balcony overlooking the water.

Kathy Knowles, always a dreamer as well as a doer, especially likes the idea of incorporating a view of the sea.

## AWARDS AND ACCOLADES

**JUNE 2013:** The Osu Children's Library Fund receives the 2013 American Library Association (ALA) Presidential Citation for Innovative International Library Projects.

**JANUARY 2012:** Kathy Knowles is named one of "Canada's 25 Transformational Canadians," a campaign sponsored by Cisco Canada, *The Globe and Mail*, CTV and *La Presse*. The award recognizes individuals *"who through their vision, leadership and action are catalysts for transformational change."*

**SEPTEMBER 2010:** The Osu Children's Library Fund receives the International Board on Books for Young People (IBBY)-Asahi 2010 Reading Promotion Award. This world-wide award is given biennially to two groups whose activities are judged to be making a lasting contribution to reading promotion for children and young people.

**JULY 2010:** Kathy Knowles receives the Order of Manitoba from the Honourable Philip S. Lee, Lieutenant Governor of Manitoba.

**JUNE 2009:** Kathy Knowles receives an Honorary Doctorate of Laws in the Field of Education, Queen's University, Kingston, ON. The citation read: *"A meticulous self-taught lay librarian who is often called upon for her wisdom as a speaker and an adviser on literacy training and library programs for children."*

**MAY 2005:** Kathy Knowles receives FLARE magazine Volunteer Award. Citation reads: *"Kathy has single-handedly enriched the lives of* *thousands of children in Ghana, West Africa. Motivating a vast contingent of volunteers, both in Canada and Ghana, she has given the lifelong tools of reading and writing to thousands of children while volunteering from the attic of her Winnipeg home."*

**AUGUST 2004:** Kathy Knowles receives the Ghanaian/Canadian Special Achievement Award, Toronto, ON.

**NOVEMBER 2002:** Kathy Knowles receives the Lewis Perinbam Award for International Development, Ottawa, ON. Citation read: *"Through her labour of love promoting literacy and education, Kathy Knowles has enriched the lives of many children half a world away and brought great honour to Canada...She has inspired communities in Canada and abroad and is a fine volunteer in the Perinbam tradition."*

**DECEMBER 2002:** Received from Robert R. Fowler, former Personal Representative of the Canadian Prime Minister for Africa, following his visit to the Nima Library, Accra, Ghana. *"Dear Kathy, It was wonderfully inspiring to see your project replace hopelessness with pride and hopefulness on the faces of so many young Ghanaians. What you have achieved through your perseverance, your inspiration and determination in promoting both education and literacy is a model for all of us and, for that, I wish to express my deepest gratitude."*

**JUNE 2001:** Kathy Knowles receives the Governor General's Meritorious Service Medal from then Governor General Adrienne Clarkson. The citation read: *"Through her labour of love promoting literacy, Kathryn Knowles has enriched the lives of many children half a world away and brought great honour to Canada."*

**MAY 2000:** Kathy Knowles receives the YMCA-YWCA Women of Distinction Award in Winnipeg, MB. This is an annual award given to a selected group of women for their contribution to the well-being of the community and for being role models to other women.

## ACKNOWLEDGEMENTS

SO MANY PEOPLE HELPED MAKE THIS BOOK HAPPEN. CLYDE SANGER, A seasoned international journalist with a long-time love of Africa, was my guide and mentor from the start and an important presence throughout.

My warmest thanks go to those who took the time to read all or parts of the manuscript at different stages along the way: Teresa de Bertodano, Wendy Blair, Theresa Morrow, Paulette Bourgeois and Christopher Cowley.

Others provided insights into both Kathy and her project: Her family —husband, John Knowles, her children—Kaitlan, Sophie, Alastair and Akos—and her parents—Beth and Gordon Lennard—all supplied information of a more personal nature. Several people in Canada also offered their comments including Richard Beatty, Ted Gale, Bruce Hildebrand, Marty Helgerson, Frank Cosway, Holly McNally, Noreen Mian, Darren Schemmer and his wife Heather Johnston, Roger Amenyogbe and Tony Jenkins while US academic, Beth Cramer, shared the findings of her PhD thesis which included laudatory comments about OCLF. A special thanks to the remarkable team of volunteers in Winnipeg, especially Joan Graham, Sally Irwin, Kathy Parry and Alice Moulton who have for years managed to keep things moving along on the home front.

In Ghana, Osu Library Fund's two directors, Emma Amoo-Gottfried and Florence Adjepong, spoke to me at length, not only about the fund's early days but about its impact on their country. Kojo MacLean, our stalwart project manager, continues to be an important member of our Ghana family while Akoss Afori-Mensah, a highly respected book publisher, filled me in on details about the publishing industry. Sara Akrofi-Quarcoo from the University of Ghana helped bring the post-election news up-to-date while Ghanaian photographer Nyani Quarmyne undertook a lengthy photo-shoot as a gift to OCLF. I am grateful as well to Mr. Hiro Hattori, formerly Chief of Education of UNICEF in Ghana, who granted me a long interview about education issues before leaving his posting in Ghana.

I must also extend my thanks to those in Ghana who help run our libraries—Joanna Felih and all the dedicated staff of our ever-expanding OCLF family. It is they who make this project the success that it is. I will long remember their friendship, their loyalty to the project and their devotion to the children they serve. My thanks as well to those library members who kindly shared their stories with me.

And a special thanks to my many personal friends who have been so supportive as the weeks and months dragged on as have my two sons, Christopher and Geoffrey, and their wives, Alena Dvorakova and Nancy Alilovic. I shamelessly add a hug for my four young grandchildren—all enthusiastic readers—who I hope will some day be able to pass on their love of books to others.

I also want to take this opportunity to remember the late Dimi Panitza, one-time European editor of the *Reader's Digest*. Dimi was a writer's dream editor who sent me to Africa on several assignments giving me my first taste of what would become a life-long love of that continent and its people.

It was due to the timely suggestion of my former editor, Rhonda Bailey, who steered me to David Carr, director of the University of Manitoba Press, who introduced me to Great Plains Publications. Ours has been a happy association and I am eternally grateful to executive editor, Ingeborg Boyens, for the confidence she showed in this project from the start and for her wisdom and patience in helping to steer it to completion.

Finally, a special bouquet goes to Kathy who spent many long hours answering my innumerable questions and, a renowned stickler for accuracy, checked hundreds of details. If any errors have managed to creep in, I take full responsibility.

—DEBORAH COWLEY, OTTAWA, JULY 2013

# INDEX